BETTER HOMES AND GARDENS®

Organize Your Home

A **Better Homes and Gardens**®Book
An Imprint of

HMH

Published by:
Houghton Mifflin Harcourt
Boston • New York
www.hmhbooks.com

For information about permission to reproduce selections from this book, write to Permissions, Houghton Mifflin Harcourt Publishing Company, 215 Park Avenue South, New York, New York 10003.

www.hmhbooks.com

Library of Congress Control Number available from the publisher upon request.
ISBN: 978-1-118-35995-2 (pbk)

Printed in the United States of America

DOW 10 9 8 7 6 5 4 3 2 1

BETTER HOMES AND GARDENS® MAGAZINE
Gayle Goodson Butler
Executive Vice President, Editor in Chief
Oma Blaise Ford
Executive Editor
Michael D. Belknap
Creative Director

BETTER HOMES AND GARDENS® ORGANIZE YOUR HOME
Editor: Samantha S. Thorpe
Contributing Editor: Brian Kramer
Contributing Designer: Kate Malo
Contributing Copy Editor: Paul Soucy
Contributing Photographers: Adam Albright, Marty Baldwin, Jay Wilde
Contributing Professional Organizers: Kathy Jenkins, Laura Leist, Lorie Marrero, Donna Smallin Kuper, Audrey Thomas
Contributing Writer: Chelsea Evers
Contributing Producer: Molly Reid Sinnett
Contributing Illustrator: Tom Rosborough
Cover Photographer: Marty Baldwin

SPECIAL INTEREST MEDIA
Editorial Director: James D. Blume
Content Director, Home: Jill Waage
Deputy Content Director, Home: Karman Hotchkiss
Managing Editor: Doug Kouma
Art Director: Gene Rauch
Group Editor: Lacey Howard
Assistant Managing Editor: Jennifer Speer Ramundt
Business Director: Janice Croat

MEREDITH NATIONAL MEDIA GROUP
President: Tom Harty
Executive Vice President: Doug Olson

MEREDITH CORPORATION
Chairman and Chief Executive Officer: Stephen M. Lacy

HOUGHTON MIFFLIN HARCOURT
Vice President and Publisher: Natalie Chapman
Editorial Director: Cindy Kitchel
Acquisitions Editor: Pam Mourouzis
Production Director: Diana Cisek
Production Manager: John Simko

bye-bye, clutter

Here's everything you need to organize every inch of your home—once and for all.

Perhaps you resolve to get organized every January 1st, or maybe you promised to finally deal with that chaotic closet after you struggled to find a favorite T-shirt. Stop spinning your wheels and start storing smartly with the no-fail strategies and techniques we've gathered into one book.

We designed Section One to lead you through the essential steps required to get motivated and successfully tackle any organizing project. Browse Section Two to tour every room in your home. You'll find small-space strategies, tips from professional organizers, before-and-after makeovers, and easy projects. And don't miss Section Three. It's packed with all the details you need to transform spaces, including how to shop for the best containers, create hardworking labels, and make over a closet.

Get ready to cure your clutter issues, store more, and stress less!

The Editors

contents

get started

Organizing is a process, not the miracle result of a product you buy. Whether you're organizing a junk drawer or your entire home, you need to go through the essential steps of successful organization before you store anything.

storage personality quiz

The best storage solutions are tailored to you and your needs.
Take our quiz, discover your personality, and find fixes
that truly suit you and your organizing challenges.

For each of the following scenarios, read all four options to see which feels most like you. Keep track of your answers to identify your organizing personality.

1. When I return from vacation and am faced with a week's worth of mail:

a. I pretend it doesn't exist and add it to the pile on the kitchen counter.

b. I take a quick peek to see whether there are any checks or coupons. I'll eventually get through the rest.

c. I take a day to unpack and settle in before sorting through it.

d. I begin sorting before my bags are unpacked, quickly tossing junk mail and setting aside important items such as bills.

2. I just realized that my daughter's soccer sign-up is tonight, but I have to attend an important meeting.

a. I assume I can be a little late to the sign-up.

b. I think to myself, *Oops, silly me. I can't believe I overlooked this.*

c. I call a neighbor whose child is also in soccer and ask her to help by signing up my daughter.

d. I think I'm losing my mind because I NEVER miss deadlines.

3. My definition of being organized is:

a. Organized? Who needs organization? I know my stuff is here somewhere.

b. If I know where my keys and my kids are, I'm organized.

c. I can usually find a document or receipt easily, even though my filing system contains only broad categories.

d. I pay my bills several days before the due date and then file my paid bills in my color-coded filing system.

4. I've been asked to say a few words during the opening ceremony of a fund-raising event.

a. I completely forget about the request and end up hastily jotting down a few words on the way to the fund-raiser.

b. I jot down a few words but lose the paper before the event—so I just wing it.

c. I prepare my remarks and neatly print them out, storing the document in a file folder until the event.

d. I spend a week researching, writing, and editing my remarks. I deliver a thought-provoking, memorized speech.

5. A friend just called. She's in the neighborhood on an errand and would like to stop by for a quick visit.

a. I look at the mess around the house and say to myself, *Who cares?* My friend loves me for who I am. She won't mind sitting next to that stack of newspapers on the sofa.

b. I love to be spontaneous with friends! I can be a little late for the PTA meeting.

c. I offer to put the coffeepot on if she'll ignore the dust.

d. I find it difficult to allow for spur-of-the-moment visits with friends. My day is too structured. Can she take a rain check?

6. My favorite activities and hobbies include:

a. Watercolor painting, pottery, and crafts.

b. Skydiving, adding to my collections, and shopping.

c. Biking, traveling, and reading.

d. Scrapbooking, gardening, and listening to music.

7. My work meeting this afternoon just got canceled. I think I will:

a. Surf online and update my Facebook and Twitter accounts.

b. Watch YouTube videos and forward the funniest to friends.

c. Check my to-do list to see if there's anything I can complete.

d. Stay focused on the project I'm currently working on. It'll be nice to get it done ahead of schedule.

8. The holidays are quickly approaching, and it's my turn to host. My first thoughts are:

a. I suppose I'll need to clear the stuff off my furniture so people won't have to sit on the floor.

b. Who wants the traditional turkey anyway? I think we should get creative and make homemade pizzas with our favorite toppings!

c. I'll create the menu and do the grocery shopping the week before, so I can avoid the crowds.

d. I'll design name cards and label each dish on the buffet line using cute tags made from my scrapbooking supplies.

9. When asked to coordinate the annual neighborhood picnic,

a. I think, *How hard could it be?*

b. I find it hard to say no. But, of course, I have no idea where to begin!

c. I say yes and then form a committee to help me with the details.

d. I gladly take it on. I create an Excel spreadsheet and assemble a binder full of notes, so I have all the details at my fingertips and can easily pass them on to next year's coordinator.

ask a pro
Our storage personalities and quiz are based on the work of professional organizer Audrey Thomas, aka Organized Audrey, who helps clients develop organization stategies that suit their personalities.

storage personality quiz

Artist

Party Planner

Teacher

Librarian

10. I was just notified that the IRS plans to audit my tax returns for the past five years. My response?

a. My accountant warned me this day might come. I've been filing extensions for several years because I just can't seem to find all the right papers.

b. As I look around at the stacks of papers in my house, I wonder whether the IRS will believe me when I say, "The dog ate it."

c. I remember putting my tax returns in a box in the basement. After a short search, I'm relieved to find them in a box labeled "Tax Returns."

d. Without hesitation or cause for concern, I go to my home safe. There, in chronological order, are my tax returns since 1986.

11. When it comes to e-mail in my in-box,

a. I have so many messages that, on occasion, I just look the other way and delete them all. If it's important, it'll come back. Won't it?

b. I am grateful for the search function and secretly pray for a system meltdown to delete the thousands of messages.

c. I create folders to hold the e-mails for my current projects and keep e-mails that need immediate attention in my in-box. While having an empty in-box is nice, it's not reality.

d. I try to make sure my in-box is nearly empty when I leave the office on Fridays. Otherwise, I won't be able to relax over the weekend.

12. It's the first of the month, and the mortgage is due along with several other bills. I think to myself:

a. Didn't I just pay last month's mortgage? Where did the time fly? And where are my current bills? I know I saw them a few weeks ago.

b. Paying bills is so boring. I'd rather take the kids to the park or watch my favorite show on TV.

c. I'll grab my bills, along with my checkbook, and pay bills while I'm waiting for the kids to complete swimming lessons.

d. No worries. Everything is set up with automatic bill pay. All I have to do is record the payments in my check register.

13. When my friends are asked to describe me, they probably use words such as:

a. Creative and artistic.

b. Spontaneous and fun-loving.

c. Predictable and structured.

d. Detail-oriented and organized.

ARTIST

You are creative and free-flowing

KEY TRAITS:

- A visual thinker and learner
- Very loyal to your friends
- Often late for appointments and sometimes unpredictable
- A pack rat

YOUR IDEAL ORGANIZING STRATEGIES:

Be realistic in the scope of your organizing projects. Instead of trying to conquer an entire room, tackle small areas such as one shelf or bar in a closet or one bookshelf. Set a timer to help you stay focused, and do as much as you can in 30 minutes. Have a reward in mind to motivate you to keep going. Look for organizing supplies that appeal to your visual nature, such as bulletin boards and open hanging file boxes.

PARTY PLANNER

You are spontaneous and fun-loving

KEY TRAITS:

- A collector
- The "fun aunt" or "fun uncle"
- Easily sidetracked
- Always striving to enjoy life and live in the moment

YOUR IDEAL ORGANIZING STRATEGIES:

Because you'd much rather be off doing fun things, you need to work hard to remain focused during an organizing project. When you begin to work in an area, make sure you have all the necessary supplies close by. Use clear plastic storage containers with lids versus open wicker baskets to corral collections and crafts—then you can see at a glance what you have rather than overbuying or forgetting about things you already own.

TEACHER

You are orderly without being excessive

KEY TRAITS:

- Predictable
- Reliable
- Structured, yet not afraid of a little spontaneity
- A rule-follower

YOUR IDEAL ORGANIZING STRATEGIES:

Getting things done on time is important to you. To prevent yourself from getting overwhelmed—and consequently overlooking important details and deadlines—break large projects into smaller chunks, assigning due dates to each step along the way. Use a three-ring binder with section dividers to help you keep track of papers related to each project.

LIBRARIAN

You like everything in its place

KEY TRAITS:

- Extremely detail-oriented
- Energetic
- A taskmaster
- A perfectionist, sometimes to a fault

YOUR IDEAL ORGANIZING STRATEGIES:

If you struggle with true perfectionism and find yourself saying, "If I can't do it perfectly, then I won't do it at all," it's time to take the pressure off. Remind yourself that having a functional home is far more important than having a perfect one. Use an electronic planner to keep your life at your fingertips. Or, if gadgets are too overwhelming, carry a paper planner.

storage personality quiz:
projects for your personality

Stop pretending to be someone you aren't! The most successful organizing comes from a place of authenticity, so do things that fit your personality and suit your deep-seated needs and desires. Work with your organizing personality to guide the types of storage projects you tackle first.

IF YOU'RE AN ARTIST

● Hang a bulletin board above a desk. Flex your creative muscles by piecing together several types of boards, including fabric-covered cork, painted pegboard, dry-erase, and chalkboard-painted.

● Tuck shallow baskets under a console table to fashion neat, easy-to-access storage for magazines. As soon as a basket is full, it's time to edit.

● Streamline the look of your clothes closet while improving function by trading in mismatched hangers for a matched set.

● Remove the doors from a few upper kitchen cabinets. The change will give the room a new look, encourage tidy habits, and let you turn everyday goods into decorative focal points.

IF YOU'RE A PARTY PLANNER

● Transform a metal cart into an entertainment station. Use office organizer drawers to hold dice and other small pieces. Corral cards in a clear container or a plastic bin.

● Evaluate where family members tend to dump their stuff as they enter the house. Then go with the flow—even if the location is the kitchen counter. Set out a catchall, such as a wicker cutlery tray, for keys, sunglasses, and electronics.

● Place shoes in clear boxes. Stack them on an eye-level shelf or higher so you can see what you have and easily access the perfect pair.

● Transform walls into organization superstars with sheets of painted pegboard, which make it simple to hang shelves and hooks and rearrange tools.

IF YOU'RE A TEACHER

● Set up a message center and in-box for each family member. Use the area to corral artwork, homework, and forms as soon as they enter your house. At week's end, go through each box, discard old materials, and file things you want to keep.

● Serve up generous file storage in style by pushing together a series of two-drawer filing cabinets to form a credenza. Unite the units with a matching coat of paint.

● Shop for several meals at once and then sort nonperishable ingredients for each into bins or baskets. Tuck a copy of the recipe into the bin, and whoever's home first can start dinner.

● Keep linens and folded clothing in line with slide-on shelf dividers and undershelf bins.

IF YOU'RE A LIBRARIAN

● Store DVD and CD cases in boxes that look good and keep things organized. Establish separate boxes for kids' movies, parents' movies, video games, and other relevant categories. Label each box so the cases get put back in the right spot.

● Establish person-specific cubbies for each family member to corral coats, bags, books, and shoes.

● Get everyone on the same page about household chores by hanging weekly to-do checklists on clipboards labeled for each person.

● Take a detailed inventory of the number of hanging clothes, bulky sweaters, folded items, shoes, and accessories you need to store. Then reconfigure your closet with the proper number and types of shelves, drawers, and rods to fit your needs.

ARTIST

PARTY PLANNER

TEACHER

LIBRARIAN

working with a pro

Frustrated with your cluttered life? Now may be the perfect time to bring in a professional to jump-start your organizing efforts.

You have the best intentions of getting organized. You've started decluttering your closet or streamlining your desk dozens of times. Maybe you've made some progress. But have you ever completed your organization projects? How much clutter—and perhaps chaos—still lingers in your home?

If the sweet experience of organizing success is eluding you, expert advice may be just what you need. Here's what you can expect from a professional organizer.

MAKING THE CASE
Many first-time home-organizing clients are skeptical about hiring someone to do what they seemingly should be able to do on their own. Cut yourself some slack. If the solution for your messy rooms was just better cleaning or putting away your stuff, you probably would be organized by now.

Ongoing clutter is a sign of something bigger. It's telling you that your situation can benefit from a fresh set of eyes, a listening ear, an inspiring voice, and a source of new ideas—all things a good professional organizer will bring to your trouble spots.

"Of course a professional's time has a cost, but how valuable is your own time?" professional organizer Lorie Marrero asks. Think about how long a project is going to take if you do it alone compared to if you have some expert help. In the end, a professional can help you do more, do it faster, and do it more thoroughly.

Finally, getting organized is work—often hard work. Knowing that a professional organizer is checking on your progress makes you accountable to someone else. That's often the motivation you need to keep going and actually finish a project.

FINDING GOOD HELP
No specific education or certifications are currently required to be a professional organizer. However,

membership in the National Association of Professional Organizers (NAPO) gives you a signal that a professional organizer is committed to helping others and running a successful, ethical business. The group's website (*napo.net*) features a searchable directory that lists more than 4,200 members throughout the United States. Just type in your ZIP code, and you'll receive a list of the options in your area.

Pay attention to areas of expertise as well as degree information or other designations in the listing. A Certified Professional Organizer (CPO) designation means a professional meets NAPO qualifications and has demonstrated knowledge through an exam and a history of client work. If you have concerns that hoarding may be part of your challenge, seek out a professional who specializes in treating that disorder.

EXPLORING YOUR OPTIONS
Just as when you hire any professional, make calls to two or three organizers. Being able to compare and contrast helps ensure you select someone who is attuned to your preferences and real needs.

For the first conversation, expect to spend around 15 minutes with each professional organizer. Remember that the professional is screening you, as well, to make sure they can help you meet your needs. As you talk, think about whether you'll be effective working with this person. Organizing can become a very intimate experience. Your organizer may see every single paper in your file cabinet, your clothing and jewelry, or your private items. You'll know after a few minutes whether the professional's style feels like a good fit.

Some professionals offer free in-person consultations or estimates in your home. These visits can be a great opportunity for the organizer to see what's really happening in your home. If that's not possible, an experienced organizer can usually learn enough about you and your project through a good phone consultation.

> ## "You are not alone. You and I can overcome this clutter. And I can teach you."
>
> —**Kathy Jenkins,** professional organizer

During the initial conversation, the professional organizer should ask about your specific project. Be prepared to describe the tasks you're struggling with—for instance, managing incoming papers, staying on top of your garage, or getting your family ready in the morning. You can also point out specific areas in your home that are giving you the greatest grief. If possible, stand in the middle of each problematic room as you describe it. Seeing the current state of the space will help you provide clearer, more specific examples for the professional to consider.

ADDRESSING MONEY MATTERS

Plan to discuss the estimated project length, fees, and rates during an initial call. Some professional organizers quote specific numbers, others don't. The most important thing is that you know what types of tasks you'll be responsible for, a range of hours potentially required from the professional, and the basic fee structure or hourly rate for calculating costs.

Realize that any estimate of a project's length depends on you—how quickly you can make decisions, how much stuff you have to physically sort through, what options you have for getting rid of items efficiently.

If you're working within a budget, share this information up front. Most professionals will work with clients' budgets, but they're probably not going to adjust their fees. Expect a smaller budget to mean less in-person time and more homework assignments. Your check-ins with the organizer may be over the phone or via e-mail, rather than in person.

At your first in-person meeting, a professional organizer should provide a service agreement for you both to sign. Agreements should protect both the client and the professional, clearly outlining confidentiality,

payment terms, basic description of the type of work to be done, and cancellation policies.

PERUSING THE PLAN

After a meeting or two, your professional organizer will likely provide you with an action plan. Each professional's approach to plans is different, but a good plan is active and clear, identifies key problems, describes actions to be taken, and recommends new routines and systems to be established.

Review your plan thoroughly and ask your professional to clarify anything you find confusing. Point out anything you anticipate will be challenging. If the plan recommends new products, make sure you know specific dimensions or materials, as well as who's responsible for acquiring the items.

MAKING PROGRESS

Good communication and collaboration are essential to successful projects. You should be clear about how and when you can contact your professional. Expect the professional to listen to your concerns along the way and transfer some skills. "We're not doing all the work for you," Marrero says. "We're teaching you how to get organized and *stay* organized."

save money

If you're motivated and budget-oriented, online consultation may be a great option for you. Do the same research as when hiring any professional and verify secure credit card and privacy practices.

If you want to get anywhere, you need a guide. A well-crafted goal is like good GPS directions that help you visualize the road ahead—and can be adjusted.

A professional organizer will usually ask you early on about your goals for a project, including which spaces you want to prioritize and how much time and money you're willing to invest in a project. If you're working on your own, you need to take the time to clarify what you hope to achieve. Here are some tips for shaping great organizing goals.

FINDING YOUR FOCUS

Professional organizer Laura Leist often begins with new clients by asking them to describe the rooms they want to organize, what their visions for the rooms are, and what is definitely *not* working for them now. "I'm listening for those pain points. You can hear it in their voices or see it in their actions," Leist says. "After I hear it, we then talk about what I heard or saw."

Try identifying some pain points on your own by standing in the middle of a room and turning slowly 360 degrees. Narrate what you're seeing at each moment. "There's the sofa. There's our favorite pillows. There's the end table . . . and there's that annoying pile of gaming gear that no ever puts away!" When you feel your pulse rise, you know you've found something specific you can better organize.

ENVISIONING THE FUTURE

Activate your brain to shape powerful organizing goals. Ask yourself why you want to get a certain room organized. "If you have a big enough reason why, that will be enough to get you going," says professional organizer Donna Smallin Kuper. Flesh out your desires with some creative thinking. What do you see this space looking like? What does "organized" look like to you? What will it feel like?

For example, close your eyes and think about that spare bedroom currently filled with piles of clutter. Ugh! Now envision what it could look like. How will you move through the room? Where will you sit or work comfortably? What will you do in the room? Hold onto that image. Write down what it looks like. Clip some inspiring images from magazines or catalogs that match your vision.

Once your brain and all your senses are fully engaged with your goal, you're ready to go.

SETTING PRIORITIES

Brainstorm a list of all the things you want to achieve in a room and try putting the items in a chronological sequence that makes sense. Avoid committing to multiple projects and goals. Strive for projects that you can complete in one work session or day, even if they're small. "You'll have the feeling of weight being lifted when you finish even a small project. Success is the biggest inspiration for further projects," Leist says.

Prioritize your projects by looking over your list of things you want to accomplish and identifying:

• **The biggest pain point.** Of all the rooms in your home, which is bothering you the most? And even more specifically, what piece of furniture or aspect of the room stands out for you? Tackle that project now.

• **The biggest payoff for the effort.** Ask yourself which project will yield the biggest results, in the shortest amount of time, with the smallest effort, and for the least amount of money. Go for that one.

to do
- ☐ sort Charlie's toys + books
- ☐ donate toys?
- ☑ clean bookcase
- ☐ buy desk
- ☐ research lights
- ☐ organize books
- ☐ 4 bins for toys:
  - blocks
  - animals
  - action
  - cars

> # "Why do you want to get organized? If you have a big enough reason why, that will be enough to get you going."
>
> —**Donna Smallin Kuper,** professional organizer

PUTTING IT IN WRITING

Turn your task list into a set of written goals. "The act of writing gets the goal into your subconscious," Leist says. "Plus, it's nice to be able to go back during and after a project to see how you're progressing."

Leist also recommends assigning a specific due date to each step and an end date for the project to reinforce the goal and shape the entire endeavor. Scheduling an important event or a party can motivate you to keep working because you want to enjoy the celebration and satisfy your guests.

If you don't have a specific event to tie to your goal, Leist recommends you still put a date on your calendar and set up a few key milestones along the way. "You must have something specific out there to work toward," she says.

GETTING REAL

Television shows about organizing and decorating distort what's possible in a day. "Clients want four-hour miracles, but they have 20 years of stuff," Leist says. You do yourself no good by pursuing a goal based on fantasy and wishful thinking. Put your goals through a reality check. Have a second pair of eyes review your goals; a neutral friend can see things you overlook.

When encountering unrealistic client goals, Leist is straightforward and tactfully suggests revisions. For instance, if you wanted to reorganize your garage in a single afternoon and work only with shelving and wall-hanging hardware you already own, she'd begin by responding positively and then bring her experience into play. She'd note what other clients can typically accomplish in three hours time and clarify the types and number of organizers you may need to purchase. She'd conclude by offering a reasonable adjustment to your original goal.

Remind yourself that you're not giving up on your original goal, you're just refining it. You didn't do anything wrong—you just learned new, important things at some point in the process.

REVISING AND REBOUNDING

Whenever barriers arise, go back and review your original goal. Ask yourself what's really keeping you from achieving your goal. A professional organizer can be extremely helpful in overcoming stalled progress.

Perhaps your goal was to have a living room where guests can sit comfortably, but several weeks into the project you're still struggling to declutter the space. Is there something going on that you need to be aware of? For example, are you actually struggling to let go of the inherited collectibles in the room that you don't really like but can't seem to deal with effectively? Take the time to craft another goal that specifically gets at the barrier you just identified.

Goal met? Reward yourself!

Having a clutter-free room—or even a perfectly organized desk drawer—feels so good, it's a reward in and of itself. But don't hesitate to consciously build in positive reinforcements. Try any of the following.

Something tasty
Knowing a sweet or salty treat awaits can keep you going for 10 to 20 minutes, which is enough time to finish boxing up donation items or stocking a pantry shelf. If you prefer more frequent refreshment, set up microtreats, such as a few chocolate chips or pretzels every time you complete the most basic of tasks.

Photo finish
After you reach a goal, take a picture. Put it on your computer desktop or phone to remind yourself of how great organization looks and feels. Share it on Facebook or via e-mail. You're sure to get an extra pat on the back for your hard work.

The big prize
Choose something to splurge on after completing a big project. Maybe it's a spa day or a new sewing machine to enjoy in your cleaned-up spare room. Pin a photo of the prize in the space where you're working to keep yourself moving forward.

breaking projects into chunks

Time and money—more specifically, the lack of one or both—are at the heart of many storage woes. Here's how to shape projects to suit your schedule or budget.

Unlimited time and money to organize your home sounds wonderful, but it's a fantasy. You have only 24 hours in a day, and, even with credit cards and loans, you probably still need to live within a budget.

When you identify what's limiting you, you're being realistic rather than negative. When you know what your limitation is, you put yourself in a better place to apply creative problem-solving and potentially work around your barriers. The following strategies help you manage your time and stretch your dollars.

IDENTIFYING STOPPING POINTS
Like most remodeling and decorating projects, big organizing projects, such as making over a closet or revamping your filing system, will not get done in a single session. You need to break big projects into a series of mini projects that you can complete in 15 to 60 minutes, depending on your stamina. This is especially true when you're strapped for time, cash, or both.

Each mini project needs a clearly defined starting and stopping point. For example, you could divide a closet into **specific functional zones** and spend chunks of time focusing only on:
- The bars for long-hanging clothing
- The bars for short-hanging clothing
- The shelves for folded clothing
- The area where you store shoes
- The area where you store accessories

Or you could divide work on the same closet into **steps you need to go through** for the entire space:
- Sorting all clothing, putting like with like
- Deciding what to keep and what to toss
- Figuring out where you want to store hanging items, folded items, and shoes in the closet
- Buying and installing new containers and hangers
- Adding labels

However you choose to break down a big project, your goal is to focus on just one area or type of task. "Having to move around or make lots of different types of decisions will wear you out quickly," says professional organizer Kathy Jenkins. Instead, Jenkins recommends defining your small projects and consciously reminding yourself as you work with something like "All I need to do right now is finish this one space" or "All I need to do for the next 15 minutes is sort clothing by type."

APPRECIATING TIME
"Many people procrastinate because they don't know how long anything actually takes," Jenkins says. To gain an accurate sense of what tasks entail, Jenkins recommends setting a stopwatch or timer and doing a specific job to completion, such as sorting the daily mail or folding a dryer load of laundry. After you recognize the fact that most daily tasks require just three to five minutes to complete, you'll be more willing to commit to keeping up with those things on a daily basis.

> "You can't overhaul your closet in an hour, but you can address just one type of clothing and end up with a clutter-free shelf or drawer. And that little spot of organization feels great every time you use it."
>
> —**Kathy Jenkins,** professional organizer

THINKING DIFFERENTLY ABOUT COSTS

How much money will you need to spend in order to park cars in your garage again or fix a meal efficiently in your kitchen? Depends.

Many successful organizing projects require no special supplies, tools, or containers. You can truly do the work yourself, reuse the stuff you have, and achieve a totally transformed space that functions beautifully without spending a cent. Or you can tackle the same project while consulting with an interior designer, commissioning new built-in cabinetry, and purchasing a flotilla of coordinating bins and baskets.

The final look and price tag will differ, but in either case you still need to do the work of organizing in order to achieve a room that works as good as it looks. You can spend money to save time (by hiring professional help) and spend time to save money (by tackling installation jobs yourself), but you can't skip doing the real work of getting organized. So carefully consider each expense, do some comparative research, and make choices that make both financial and functional sense.

FINDING TIME, FINDING MONEY

You're only as poor as you believe yourself to be. Take 20 minutes and make an inventory of the time and money resources you have available.

To plan your time resources, look at a calendar and note the weekends, evenings, and vacation time you have available. Estimate how many hours you are willing to spare each week to getting organized. You can choose to spend a few minutes, several hours, or all your free time. There's no right answer. Just determine ahead of time what makes sense for you, then schedule your commitment in your planner.

Start to plan your budget by looking at your checkbook and savings and identifying how much money you can—and, more important, *want*—to dedicate to paying professionals and purchasing products. Stretch your budget by:

• selling items you no longer want or need
• asking an honest friend to help with time-draining decisions or physically exhausting moving
• trading skills and services with friends and neighbors
• assigning projects or tasks to other family members

MAKING THE OLD NEW

You'll see the word "repurpose" frequently throughout this book, and for good reason. The process of using things you already have, just in different ways, makes sense on many levels.

Repurposing forces you to think creatively and eliminate preestablished notions. So what if a bamboo box you own was originally designed to hold CDs? If you no longer need to organize discs, the bin might be the perfect size to keep all your hair care products standing tall, plus the wood's water-resistant qualities are ideal for the bathroom. By reassigning storage duties, you gain a great new container and avoid tossing a well-made but no longer essential item.

Making the most of 15 minutes

You can become more organized in 15 minutes, but only when you clearly define your projects. Consider tackling any of the following bite-size projects the next time you have a free quarter-hour:

- Junk drawer
- Cooking- or eating-utensil drawer
- Spice rack
- One pantry shelf
- Freezer
- Refrigerator
- Jewelry
- Cosmetics or grooming supplies
- Medicine cabinet
- Linen closet
- One type of clothing
- One bookshelf
- Main desk drawer
- Undersink area in kitchen, bath, or utility room
- Storage above or around the washer/dryer
- Car glove box
- Car trunk
- Purse or other personal bag
- Wallet

Don't have 15 minutes to spare? Think again. The typical hour-long television program includes 17 minutes of commercials (and as much as 23 minutes during late-night shows). Get a DVR to record shows and make the most of the minutes you gain speeding through ads.

decluttering & editing

Before you store anything, make
sure you really want to keep it.
Follow our foolproof approach
to streamlining your stuff.

Decluttering is the essential (and yet often forgotten) step of any storage makeover. When you declutter, you take the time to assess every item hanging in your closet, piling on your desktop, or filling that kitchen junk drawer. You look closely at your stuff, deciding to keep some things and let go of others. The process is vital because, in the end, you want to store only the stuff that you actually use or love.

The biggest challenge when decluttering is the tendency to set too ambitious a goal. Rather than taking on an entire room, focus on just one corner, a key piece of furniture, or a particularly messy drawer or cabinet. Remember, your goal is to build up your confidence and decision-making skills so you can move on to bigger things. See "Breaking projects into chunks" *on page 18* for more on managing large organizing projects.

> "If you have clutter, you're richer than you think. Clutter is physical proof of our abundance. Things are obligations. Letting go releases you from obligation."
>
> —**Donna Smallin Kuper,** professional organizer

GETTING READY TO CLUTTER-BUST

"Decluttering can be a roller coaster of emotions, so plan ahead and cut yourself some slack," says professional organizer Kathy Jenkins. Dress in comfortable clothes, put on some energetic music, and have a favorite beverage or snack on hand.

You'll make better decisions when you can work uninterrupted, so schedule a decluttering session in advance. "Write it down like an appointment, and honor it like you would a doctor or dentist appointment," says professional organizer Donna Smallin Kuper. Minimize disruptions by letting family know ahead of time when you'll be busy.

PLAYING BEAT THE CLOCK

Jenkins recommends starting with a three-hour decluttering session, but you may be able to work up to five hours or so successfully. If you're concerned about your stamina, commit to a few one-hour sessions spread over several consecutive days.

Whatever the length of time, take breaks every 30 minutes to assess how things are going. Set a timer or use music to keep yourself on schedule.

AVOIDING THE EVERYDAY

While you may be tempted to dive into your home's "clutter hot spots," such as a desk or the kitchen cabinets, focus first on areas that you don't use often, such as a linen closet or a supply cabinet. These areas are probably bursting with unnecessary items, so you can achieve the satisfaction of gathering lots of things to donate or discard. Also, if necessary, you can stop working on these types of areas for a day without inconveniencing yourself or your family.

TOUCHING THINGS ONCE—OR NOT AT ALL

Go through any space you're decluttering in a methodical way: left to right, high to low, front to back—whatever makes the most sense for your project. Pick up each item and assess it. Try on articles of clothing. Test tools and electronics to see if they work. Verify that you have all the pieces of games, kits, and sets. Then decide if the item is a keeper or not. Use the questions in the sidebar "Asking the tough questions," *right,* to help make decisions.

If you're decluttering items that have emotional connections (clothing, jewelry, inherited collectibles), Smallin Kuper recommends having a neutral person help by holding up the item and asking you whether you want to keep it. By not having a physical connection to Grandma's teacups or your high school graduation gown, you'll actually be in a better state of mind to make clear decisions.

THINKING DIFFERENTLY

To make decluttering as painless as possible, shift your thinking. Jenkins recommends replacing self talk like "I have to get rid of this item" with phrases such as "I'm parting company with this item," "Someone else will really enjoy this great item," or "I'm keeping the best of the best."

decluttering & editing

You've ruthlessly assessed your stuff and separated out the items you're keeping, and you've immediately returned everything that belongs to someone else.

So now what do you do with the things you no longer need? While your options vary depending on where you live and the services available, here are your main options.

1. SELL IT
Your first notion may be to host a garage sale or sell your stuff on Craigslist or eBay. Wait just a second! Do you truly have the time and energy to sell things in the next few days? If not, move on to other options. You don't want a spare room of things you'll sell someday.

2. GIVE IT AWAY
If you know of someone specific who can use an item, contact him or her immediately. Do not keep things because you're sure that someone somewhere will want the item someday. If you don't know a specific person now, move on to other options.

Consider free exchange networks. For example, the Freecycle Network (*freecycle.org*) has hundreds of grassroots, non-profit groups around the world. Each local group is moderated online by local volunteers; membership is free. The network provides individuals and non-profits an electronic forum to "recycle" unwanted items. Simply send an e-mail offering an item to members of your local Freecycle group.

3. DONATE IT
Most national donation-accepting organizations and charities (such as Goodwill, Salvation Army, St. Vincent de Paul, and others) are interested only in items that are new, unused, or in excellent condition. If you don't have any use for a beaten-up armchair or a broken stove, the charity probably won't either.

Visit *CharityNavigator.org* for detailed evaluations of thousands of charities in the United States and abroad. You'll also find links to charities in your area and Q&As on how donating affects your taxes.

4. RECYCLE OR DISPOSE OF IT
If you can't find a person, organization, or charity that can use your item, it's time to (ideally) recycle the item or dispose of it.

Visit *Earth911.org* to find your best options for recycling or disposing of items. Simply enter the items you're getting rid of (tires, appliances, electronics, furniture, and so on) and your ZIP code, and the site lists your options based on proximity to your home. Contact information is available for most options, so you can find out what you need to do to drop off your stuff or arrange for a pickup.

Tricky stuff and what to do with it

BOOKS
- Your local library may want used books to add to their collection or to sell at fund-raisers.
- Books for Soldiers ships books to U.S. soldiers deployed around the world; paperbacks preferred.
- Books to Prisoners mails your old books to prisoners.

BUILDING SUPPLIES & APPLIANCES
- Habitat for Humanity's ReStores accept reusable and surplus building materials and appliances. Proceeds help fund Habitat homes.

CELL PHONES
- Cell Phones for Soldiers sells old phones to a recycling company and uses proceeds to buy calling cards for soldiers.
- Wireless Foundation's Donate a Phone program enables local organizations to collect used wireless phones, with proceeds serving as a fund-raiser for the local organizations.
- Verizon Wireless refurbishes phones for use by domestic violence survivors.

CLOTHING
- Dress for Success provides professional clothes to women for job interviews.
- Career Gear helps outfit men who need professional and business casual clothing for job interviews.
- Your local shelter for abused women may be grateful for clothing.

COMPUTERS & ELECTRONIC WASTE
- Electronics Recycling and Earth 911 lead you to local recyclers and refurbishers.

EYEGLASSES
- The Lions Club has a long history of helping people who need glasses get them. Check the Lions Club website to find a drop-off location near you.

MUSIC, GAMES, MOVIES
- Swap.com is an online marketplace where millions of members trade music, games, and movies.

PROM DRESSES
- Donate My Dress provides formal dresses to girls who otherwise won't have a gown for the ball.
- Smashion lets you sell still-trendy clothes online with no fees (buyers pay the shipping costs).

SHOES
- Soles4Souls distributes good-condition shoes to those in need.

TOWELS, LINENS, RUGS
- Animal shelters and humane societies use old linens and sometimes rugs to provide comfort to animals. Call your local ASPCA, Humane Society, or small-animal rescue group.

TOYS & STUFFED ANIMALS
- Stuffed Animals for Emergencies distributes used toys to emergency organizations, children's services, hospitals, and homeless shelters.

sorting & putting stuff away

Before you restock a shelf or put anything in a container, you need to know the type and amount of stuff you have. Then you can put it away.

If you've decluttered and you're still looking at an imposing pile of clothing, kitchen goods, or toiletries, use the SIMPLE method, professional organizer Kathy Jenkins' acronym for the six essential steps of organizing:

S: Sort like with like.
I: Identify what to keep.
M: Make a home for it.
P: Put it in containers.
L: Label it.
E: Establish a routine.

"The SIMPLE method is all about acting rather than overthinking," Jenkins says. Making dozens of decisions haphazardly about what to keep, where to keep it, and how to label it will wear you out quickly. The SIMPLE method structures the process. You're just following steps, not reinventing the wheel.

CREATING CATEGORIES: A SORTING ESSENTIAL
Take a quick look over the items you have to organize and create a list of "sort categories." You may need to sort your pile by room, by person, by function, by type, or in some other manner. At first, writing down categories may seem obvious or silly, but you're trying to make things as easy as possible for yourself. Specific spaces often require specific sort categories. In a pantry, you encounter baking supplies, spices, mixes, snacks, and so on. The sort categories in your garage or guest bedroom will be totally unique. Bottom line: Your categories must make sense to you and for the items you need to sort.

Jenkins recommends writing each sort category on an index card or half-sheet of paper. Spread the cards out on a tabletop, bed, or swath of floor to serve as temporary labels for new piles you create.

KEEPING —RATHER THAN PURGING
After sorting, you identify what to you truly want to keep. You're doing more than decluttering. "The trick here is to remain positive," Jenkins notes. "Focus on deciding what's important to you rather than what to purge."

As you're sorting into piles:

- **Eliminate** duplicate and broken items.
- **Further edit down** to the best or most frequently used items.
- **Move** piles that belong elsewhere to more appropriate locations and plan to deal with them later.

See the sidebar "Asking the tough questions" *on page 21* for helpful tips to further smooth the sorting process.

MAKING A HOME FOR EVERYTHING

You're ready to start putting things away, but now you're going to put them away with *purpose*. If decluttering is about streamlining your stuff, then purposing is about getting specific about where your stuff should live.

"If you don't define exactly how you use things, you'll end up with a mess," professional organizer Audrey Thomas says. "Maybe not the day after decluttering but certainly in the weeks to follow."

BEING GUIDED BY FREQUENCY

To create purposeful storage, ask how and how often you use a specific item. Your answer gives you clues about how to store stuff and set up spaces for optimal function. For example, your monthly credit card bill is more than a piece of paper. It's a reminder that you need to write a check (or electronically transfer funds) before the due date. Rather than dumping the bill on your desk, place it where you'll see it. For convenience, it should be near your checkbook or computer and any mailing supplies. Storing the bill purposefully may mean pinning it in a specific spot on a bulletin board or clipping it in a desktop stand labeled "To Pay."

"There is no set place where an item should be stored. Your decisions of where to store something must be based on how frequently you use it," says professional organizer Laura Leist. Take a waffle iron, for example. For many people, waffles are special treats that they make two or three times a year, so the iron can be stored on an upper pantry shelf or in the cabinet above the refrigerator. But if your Sunday tradition is a waffle brunch, you need to store this appliance in a prime spot, perhaps in the pullout drawer of a cooking island.

sorting & putting stuff away

ZONING

A strategically zoned space is an extension of purposeful placement. Analyze and break down any space into several functional areas, each with specific duties. A chaotic home office might include major subsections such as a filing cabinet, desktop, bookcase, and other essential furniture pieces. Examine each of the zones and define it down to the smallest element; the top drawer of the filing cabinet becomes the space for current contracts and correspondence to be answered, while the second drawer is home to budgets and frequently referenced reports, and so on.

BRINGING IN THE GANG

Of course, real life involves other people. After considering your own organizational needs, expand your purposeful planning to include other people in your home. How do others use specific items or spaces? What are their expectations? How are these expectations different from yours?

Families have lots of expectations about common-use areas, such as mudrooms, coffee tables, or kitchen counters. These expectations are often in conflict—one parent wants to use the kitchen counter to prepare dinner, the other parent wants to sort mail there, and a child wants to spread out homework. "Everyone is right in how they're using the counter because it's in a common-use area," Thomas says. "Problems arise because the counter hasn't been defined for everyone." A set of baskets—one for each family member—could encourage flexibility and personal responsibility. Or a schedule with set times for homework, meal prep, and other common tasks could clarify who gets first dibs on a common resource.

FINESSING YOUR PRIME STORAGE SPOTS

When you stand or sit near your home's hardest-working zones—your bathroom vanity, entry closet, desk, or meal prep area—the best storage spots are at eye level. Dedicate these areas to the things you use

> ## "Question everything! Just because you store something one way right now doesn't mean it has to be stored in that location or in that way forever."
>
> —**Donna Smallin Kuper,** professional organizer

most. You should be able to see each essential item and reach it with minimal effort or movement.

After you restock these areas, test-drive them for a week and consider how quickly and easily you're able to get the stuff you need. Revise your storage plan if you need to strain to reach anything or find your use interrupted by other objects, people, or traffic patterns.

KEEPING AN EYE ON THINGS

When deciding where to store items, think about what you need to see and what you don't. Items you use daily should be stored in your handiest storage spots. A single barrier between you and the item, such as a cabinet door or a box lid, is fine. But open storage spots, such as shelves, counters, and desktops, are typically the most important spots to thoughtfully organize.

Professional organizer Lorie Marrero recommends that anything that you use daily follow the acronym VEO (which is Spanish for "I see"). These solutions must be:

> **V:** Visible
> **E:** Easy to use
> **O:** Obvious to everyone

Thus, you and your entire family are much more likely to put away shoes on a shelf or drop them in a bin in the entry than open a lidded shoe bench (not visible), work a spinning shoe rack (not easy), or stash them in the drawers of a vintage armoire (not obvious).

Reinforce VEO by choosing transparent containers (*see page 234* for ideas) and adding meaningful labels (*pages 242–245*).

planning your purchases

There's no shortage of stores, websites, and catalogs dedicated to cool storage products. Here's how to pick the best solutions for your space.

Just a moment, excited storage shopper. Put down that credit card! Before you buy, you need to make certain that you're purchasing the best solution for your situation. The following tips ensure your new acquisitions meet your expectations.

KEEPING IT SIMPLE

Putting stuff in containers is actually the *fourth* step of Kathy Jenkins' six-step SIMPLE method (*see page 24*), contrary to many people's instinct to buy new furniture or containers and get organized later. "Buying first often forces a solution on you," Jenkins says. It's also very likely to waste your money, or at the very least require you to spend time returning purchases.

Realize that it's OK to not have the perfect container right now. Use what you have on hand. Repurpose extra desk organizers in a bath vanity or file documents in a banker's box for a while. Even cut-down cereal boxes and plastic baggies can set your new organizing plan in motion while you await new containers. "Take good measurements and do some research. Eventually you will find it," Jenkins says.

EVALUATING THOROUGHLY

When you find a product that seems absolutely perfect, professional organizer Lorie Marrero recommends asking five key questions:

- **Will it last?** If possible, examine the construction and the materials used. Will it stand up to daily use or multiple users?
- **Will you really use it?** Imagine yourself using the product, or better yet, test it in the store. Walk through the steps of how you plan to actually interact with it.
- **Does it improve visibility?** Aside from containers for long-term storage, you need to be able to see the items being organized fairly easily. "Simply put, if you're going to use it, you need to see it," Marrero says.
- **Will it fit?** Take thorough measurements of your space and any nearby furnishings or features that may

be relevant, such as windows, doors, or columns. (See the sidebar "Measuring accurately" for tips.) Double-check the new product's dimensions yourself in the store, if possible.

● **Is it easy to maintain?** Choose products made of scrubbable materials and featuring machine-washable fabric. Lots of curves and carved details will slow down your cleaning.

If you answer no to any of these questions but are still interested in the item, get a second opinion from a friend or a professional organizer. A neutral person can cut through the marketing and hype, evaluating a product's true merits or faults.

OPTIMIZING OPEN STORAGE

Open bookcases and shelves do not automatically organize a room. In fact, bookcases stocked without the aid of a strategic plan and a few accessories often make a room look more cluttered. To tame vast shelves, plan to incorporate a mix of the following products.

● **Baskets and bins** are ideal for corralling stuff you drop off or pick up often, such as toys, gloves, or shoes.
● **Lidded boxes** gather small items in one spot and can mask less-than-lovely contents. Because you must remove the lid to access what's inside, these containers are best for items you interact with less frequently.
● **Magazine files** help slim publications stand up vertically. They're useful for organizing more than periodicals, such as children's books, paperbacks, notebooks, folders, and even loose papers.
● **Dividers and bookends** introduce order to horizontal expanses, letting you dedicate areas to specific topics or types of items.
● **Risers** add extra layers of vertical storage to shelves and keep smaller objects—spice containers, toiletries, or collections—from getting lost.

The exact dimensions, shapes, and materials of all these products vary widely. Take thorough measurements of both your shelves and the new organizers before purchasing.

MAKING WAY

Furniture needs to fit your square footage—and you need to fit, too! Allow adequate clearance around pieces so you can use them effectively.

● **Interior doors** require a 3-foot arc on the side they open to operate properly.
● **Walkways** around a room (and around a bed) should be at least 30 inches wide.
● **Distance between** upholstered seating and a coffee table ranges from 14 to 18 inches.
● **Dining and desk chairs** need about 36 inches of pullout space behind them.
● **Cabinet doors and drawers** require 36 inches of clearance space for comfortable use.

KNOWING THE STANDARDS

Although the upholstered furniture available today comes in a range of lengths, depths, and heights, measurements for key storage pieces are fairly consistent. Of course, always check the actual dimensions of any element you already own:

● **Bookcases** are typically 9 to 12 inches deep. Cases with measurements outside this range are usually custom or pieces specifically designed to hold media or office equipment.
● **Two-drawer file cabinets** are approximately 29 inches high and 28½ inches deep. The width is 15 inches with letter-size drawers, 18¼ inches with legal-size. Smaller cabinets are available, but they don't have fully extendable drawers, so you'll sacrifice convenience.
● **Standard kitchen base cabinets** measure 24 inches deep and approximately 36 inches high with countertop.
● **Traditional bathroom base cabinets** are 30 inches high, but many people now prefer taller kitchen cabinets in baths.
● **Windowsills** are typically 18 to 36 inches from the floor. Benches, desks, and storage cubes are best options for storage in front of windows.
● **Tables and desks** are typically 28 to 30 inches tall. A comfortable work space is at least 30 inches wide.

establishing successful routines

Reinforce the hard work you've done to conquer clutter with labels, reminders, and other tools to keep yourself on track.

School

Finances

Medical

Taxes

"Your routine should be whatever you need to remind you of what you're supposed to do."

—**Kathy Jenkins,** professional organizer

Getting organized feels great, and staying organized feels even better. Whether you worked hard to achieve a clutter-free closet or just a streamlined sock drawer, make organization an easy, ongoing experience with the following tips.

GETTING IN THE HABIT

Whatever you call it—your system, your routine, or your habit—it's incredibly important. It's how you do things time after time in your home.

"Your routine should be whatever you need to remind you of what you're supposed to do," professional organizer Kathy Jenkins says. Successful routines can (and should) be very simple:

• A sticky note on top of your planner reminding you about today's important activities.
• A house rule to "Put it back when you're done."
• A practice of opening the mail over a trash basket every evening when you come home.

The best routines simply extend existing behaviors, so look for ways to add a final organizing flourish to things you already do. For example, after brushing your teeth at night, organize your vanity by placing your toothbrush in a hygienic holder. Doing so takes just as much effort as leaving the brush by the sink, and the extra action feels like a fitting conclusion to your day.

MAKING IT VISUAL

The best tools to establish and reinforce systems are simple: notes, checklists, and schedules. Electronic versions of all these exist, but if you like the physical satisfaction of writing a list or marking off items, stick with paper. And don't underestimate the power of a few good labels! Labels are your go-to tool for establishing new systems, teaching others where things go, and training yourself and others in new habits.

Your labels don't need to be perfect or fancy, just accurate and helpful. Professional organizer Donna Smallin Kuper encourages clients to create temporary labels with sticky notes and come back later and create nice labels. "Decluttering is a never-ending process," Smallin Kuper says, "but labeling is something you do and you're done. So just make the label now. And whatever you do will probably work." Turn to pages 242–245 for more on labels.

MAKING CHANGES

Routines don't last forever, so regularly examine yours and be open to revisions. "The project of getting organized is short," Jenkins says. "But the process of staying organized is much longer. Think of it as an ongoing assessment. Ask yourself what's working and what's not working often."

Pay particular attention to the number of steps in any routine. Is it possible to reduce your effort, combine a few steps, or eliminate some steps altogether—while still achieving the same result? Perhaps sorting recyclables after every meal made sense with a young family 10 years ago, but now as an empty nester and with the advent of single-stream recycling, you may be better off collecting empties in a small bin under the sink for several days and then tossing that in a bigger bin in your garage.

Hire a professional organizer or ask a friend to watch you go through your typical process of sorting laundry or getting ready in the morning. An outside observer simply asking "Why?" can yield surprising insights.

staying motivated

Don't sweat it if your best-made plans occasionally go awry. Everyone encounters obstacles along the way to a more organized life. Get back on your feet and moving forward with these tips.

I Did It!

The obstacles that stand between you and an organized home may seem totally unique and insurmountable. But others have gone through what you're experiencing right now. What worked for them can work for you. Figure out which of the following four organizing hurdles you're encountering, and make a few minor changes to turn things around. Here's what to do if you're struggling with:

Feeling Overwhelmed

ATTITUDE:
"There's just too much to tackle. I don't have the time or energy."

SOLUTION:
Come up with a plan and a timeline for taking it one step at a time.

TURN-IT-AROUND TACTICS
Feeling overwhelmed is a frequently cited reason for seeking the help of a professional organizer. If this sounds familiar, focus on simple solutions:

• Examine the room you want to organize and visually break it into small areas that you can tackle in increments. Set achievable deadlines to give yourself a goal to work toward.

• Make a list of what absolutely stays and what could go to reduce clutter. Writing things down transforms organization from a dream to a plan.

• Focus on the reason for reorganizing, such as cleaning out a guest room so you have space for visitors. Or, if negative reinforcement motivates you, picture how a space will look if you take no action: mounds of unsorted mail piled to the ceiling. Yuck!

• Prioritize your tasks, starting in an area where you can quickly see progress.

• Schedule time to work on a project when you're most energetic and least likely to be distracted. Set a timer and quit when the timer rings.

Attachment

ATTITUDE:
"I can't get rid of these things. They belonged to a loved one, or I might need them in the future."

SOLUTION:
Keep only the things that really matter to you, that you use, and that you have room for.

TURN-IT-AROUND TACTICS
Sentimental attachments—whether to jewelry, furniture, clothing, or old letters—are hard to break. Emotions relating to a divorce, death, or estrangement can make it challenging to examine items and determine what to keep and what to let go.

• Ask a trusted friend to help you go through memorabilia. It's easy to get lost in the past while going through old letters or photos. A friend will keep you on track.

• Ask a friend to presort items. Dealing with sorted piles makes it easier to make decisions.

• Be kind to yourself and give yourself more time to tackle objects that have feelings attached to them. But don't let grief or guilt bully you into keeping things you don't really need. Keep only a few strong sentimental reminders.

• Remember that getting rid of stuff doesn't have to mean throwing items away. Giving your extras to others in need can give you a tax deduction as well as a sense of satisfaction.

Procrastination

ATTITUDE:
"I don't have the time or energy today, so I'll handle it later."

SOLUTION:
Make yourself accountable by setting deadlines. Reward yourself when you achieve your goals.

TURN-IT-AROUND TACTICS
Stalled decision-making and lack of action are at the heart of disorganization. Kick-start your makeover with these solutions:

• Find a motivation partner. Set a day and time each week to talk about what you want to get done and how you plan to do it. Being accountable to someone else is a powerful motivator—you are more likely to follow through with your to-do list if you have to explain why you didn't.

• Reward and/or discipline yourself, depending on what motivates you most. You might reward yourself by eating out at a favorite restaurant or getting a spa treatment. Or you might give yourself a reality check by getting up early for a few days to achieve your goal.

• Throw a party. If you shift into organizational overdrive when company's coming, schedule events in your home.

• If you respond to visuals, try prominently displaying photos of disorganized spaces alongside magazine photos that illustrate how you want your space to look.

Perfectionism

ATTITUDE:
"If I can't do it right, I won't do it at all."

SOLUTION:
Get started, do the best you can in the time you have, and accept that everything is not perfect.

TURN-IT-AROUND TACTICS
Perfection is an impossible goal. Focus on success and ongoing improvement instead:

• Come up with an organizational plan that works for now, knowing that you can tweak the plan later.

• Recognize that the most important thing is just getting started. Begin with a small, manageable project, such as a sock drawer. Every morning when you find a pair of matched socks, you'll be inspired to tackle organizing additional drawers and other spaces. Experiencing the benefits of organization breeds motivation.

• Choose progress, not perfection. Repeat to yourself that almost perfect is good enough, and keep moving forward. Don't get bogged down in details that don't really matter.

room by room

Big projects become manageable when you break them into smaller parts. The following nine chapters help you identify the spaces in your home most in need of organizing and offer targeted solutions that yield major results.

2:00 Dance Recital

Saturday
Soccer Practice 10:30
At Newton Park

Milk
Butter
Pasta

entries

If life is a series of entrances and exits, the area inside your home's door is where a whole lotta living happens. Finesse this zone for great beginnings and endings.

Stop stumbling and stressing as you enter or exit your home by considering three key questions. **Who uses the entrance?** Figure out who most frequently passes through each door and implement solutions that satisfy the specific needs of family, guests, or a combination of the two. **Where do you naturally drop stuff?** Rather than fighting your habits, work with them. For example, adding a sturdy bookcase for collecting bags at an entry may be a better approach than pleading with others to pick up after themselves. **What do you need to access quickly?** You can't store every pair of shoes near the door—and you don't need to. Prioritize just the pair or two you wear most often.

ultimate entry

This transitional zone maintains user-friendly function with smart shelving, labeled bins, and drop spots for mail and keys.

A BUILT-IN THAT'S 14 inches deep incorporates a bench and a locker-style compartment for coats. Matching containers on the top shelf hold less-used items such as pet gear, sports equipment, and gardening supplies.

Spray-painted bins *above, far left* **assist in sorting recyclables. The handled containers can be quickly emptied into a larger receptacle in the garage for pickup day.**

Creative labeling *below, far left* **adds a fun twist to maintaining order. Removable glue dots designed for scrapbooking layouts hold letter tiles in place, so labels can be revised when contents change.**

A galvanized organizer *left* **organizes outgoing mail, wallets, sunglasses and wristlet purses. Labeled hooks ensure keys don't get mixed up.**

Choose sturdy, scrubbable bins for storing sports equipment, pet needs, and gardening supplies.

in the zone

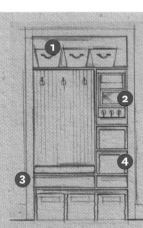

1 The top shelf holds bins of seasonal items, such as gardening tools and sports gear, that aren't used daily.

2 Small hooks on a galvanized mail organizer hold keys, wallets, and small personal bags.

3 A shallow shelf is home to a few pairs of shoes, while a bench serves as spot to lace up.

4 Baskets corral hats, scarves, and gloves. A folded blanket at the ready on a lower shelf is great for car trips or picnics.

small-space drop zone

Cleverly combined furnishings elevate a basic wall to a dynamic drop zone for daily essentials.

returns

shopping bags

pay

A BUREAU WITH open shelves welcomes shoes on its lowest level and bins filled with reusable shopping bags and to-be-returned library books.

A lidded basket *above, far left* **tucks cold-weather accessories under a wall-hugging bench. As seasons change, so can the contents and labels.**

Wall-mount cubes *below left* **hold essentials clustered by function, including grooming items, note-taking tools, and several pairs of sunglasses.**

A footed ceramic bowl *left* **acts as an attractive, low-tech charging station. A converted lunch box contains a digital camera and all its accessories. A small dish nearby houses jewelry and pocket contents until the next trip out the door.**

Because you're usually carrying things as you enter and exit, drop-zone solutions need to be accessible with one hand.

small smarts

1 Modular cubbies corral sunglasses, makeup, and supplies for jotting down quick notes.

2 A key tree and a lunch box filled with photography supplies are quirky grab-and-go solutions.

3 A wall rack with five hooks holds essential gear for several family members.

4 A comfy bench softens the hardworking space while providing room for storage underneath.

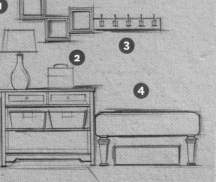

essential elements

Even with limited floor space, you can stop clutter at the door by adding these four must-haves to your entry area.

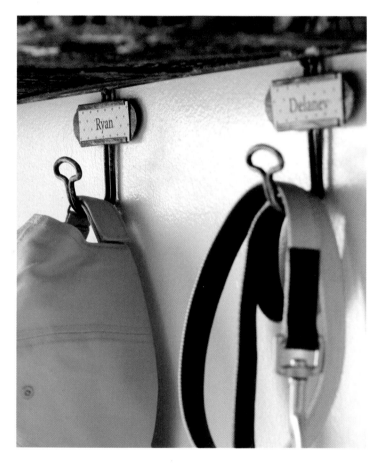

HOOKS

"Using a hook should be as easy as tossing your coat over a chair or on the floor," professional organizer Donna Smallin Kuper says. "And when a solution is easy, you're much more likely to maintain your clutter-free life." Install the right number and type of hooks by first editing down to the items you wear daily and supplying hooks for only these items. Test-drive a hook's placement before drilling by running through how you'll hang items on it and remove items later.

COMMUNICATION SOLUTIONS

Even in an age of e-mails and texts, busy families benefit from written notes, paper forms, and printed schedules. Establish a spot for dropping off and picking bits of information. You're not setting up a full-service home office, just installing some type of memo board, designating official drop spots or mailboxes for each family member, and stocking some basic note-taking supplies. Don't forget to include a small trash bin to gather junk mail the moment it enters your home.

Each new season gives you a chance to evaluate how and what you store in your entry.

OPEN STORAGE

Open shelves and compartments usually make more sense in an entry area than lots of doors, handles, and latches, which block you from quickly putting things in their proper places. Open solutions are also more flexible than closed. "Your system can grow with your family," Smallin Kuper says. "The same basic unit can accommodate baby gear early on, then move on to organizing gym bags and sporting equipment later with just a few container changes."

SHOE ORGANIZING SOLUTION

Stop fighting it: Shoes are a fact of life. Begin to embrace reality with moppable flooring and washable rugs or mats inside and outside your door. Decide on the number of shoes each family member may keep in the entry area and enforce your policy with a nightly purge. Rather than dumping frequently worn footwear in a seemingly bottomless basket, Smallin Kuper recommends resting pairs on an expandable tiered rack or shelf, which gets shoes off the ground to air-dry.

challenges | personal gear

Take control of shoes, sports equipment, and outerwear in your home's busiest hubs.

Regularly audit the stuff that crowds your entry areas. Ask yourself what belongs in this space— and what doesn't belong. For example, sporting equipment often ends up in entries, but the garage may be a better place because you can install specialty organizers there.

If kids are involved, rely on open storage. "'Your cubby' and 'your hook' are what they learn in kindergarten," professional organizer Donna Smallin Kuper says. "You almost don't need to teach your kids to use these solutions at home."

Prevent last-minute panic by designating a bin or basket for each member of the family to drop keys and wallets in.

1. ON THE BENCH
A small storage bench becomes a hub for sports equipment when labeled baskets are added to cubbies. Key-tag labels sort gear by name.

2. CATCHY IDEA
Too tired to look through mail and important papers when you walk through the door? A tray keeps incoming documents together until you're ready to respond.

3. CARRIED AWAY
Fill a bookcase with metal pails to store gear. Magnets secure helpful reminders and notes between family members.

4. DOUBLE UP
Stacking containers maximize limited floor space along an entry wall. Stow less-used items in the bottom containers, and purses, backpacks, and other everyday essentials in the top bins. Casters let you slide a stack from room to room.

5. ROLL CALL
Give parents and kids maximum storage space with locker units. Monogrammed bins on upper shelves hold personal items and serve as nameplates. The drawers below the bench seat are ideal for everyday items, while the pullout shoe trays implement a two-pairs-per-person policy.

challenges | mail & communication

Stay connected without the clutter. Here's how to better manage mail, to-do lists, and all those electronics.

You're often in a hurry and loaded up with bags and other gear as you enter and exit your home, so opt for super-simple communication systems. Memo boards, sorters, and mailboxes are classic tools to share messages in entries, but avoid overshopping. Test one system at a time for one to two weeks to see how your family responds. Keep your message system lean and meaningful by nightly delegating outstanding to-do items and removing all completed or extraneous notes.

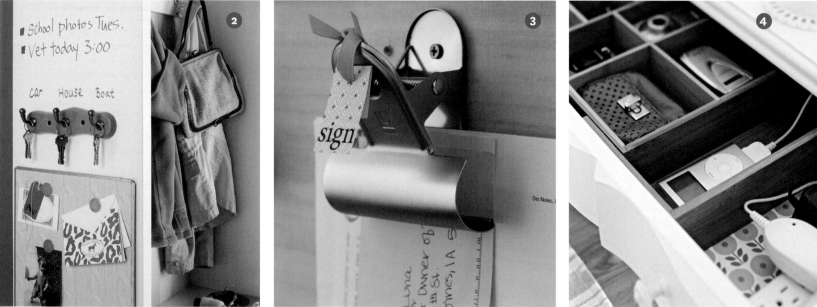

When implementing a new communication tool, take time to explain it to your family so they're on board.

PEDIATRICIAN · 404·555·4595

MAGNUS CELL · 404·555·9748
             404-555-7136
ILI CELL · 404·555·8189
EVY+BENGT · 904·555·0087
MICHI CELL · 787·555·7672
BENGT CELL · 904·555·1274
ANIMAL POISON —888·555·4435

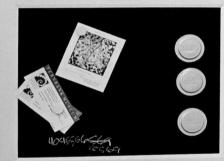

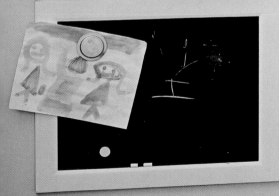

save time

Stop forgetting lunches, musical instruments, or other essential items when you leave for the day by affixing a note to the door frame or hanging a related item on a hook near the door to trigger your memory.

1. TURN AROUND

A spinning carousel organizer gathers mail and memos by person or topic as soon as they come through the door. Small drawers hold stamps and address labels for on-the-go mailing.

2. THE WRITE STUFF

Coat a wall or portion of cabinetry with dry-erase paint to create an unconventional memo board. Below the key rack, a cookie sheet covered in adhesive paper serves as a magnetic surface for posting invitations and school papers.

3. ON THE GO

Fasten a bulldog clip to a wall near the door for outgoing mail, permission slips, and anything else that needs immediate attention.

4. PLUGGED IN

A wood utensil tray gets a makeover when drilled to accommodate chargers. A power strip in the back of the drawer charges phones, cameras, and music devices, while adjacent cubbies tidy keys and wallets.

5. ALL ABOARD

Inexpensive framed chalkboards hung together create a memo center. Low boards are perfect for showcasing kids' art, upper boards for important info for older family members.

challenges | pets & weather

When you plan ahead, mucky boots and muddy paws are manageable nuisances rather than total chaos.

Your goal is to get wet, dirty footwear off your feet—and off your floor—as quickly as possible. A bench or stool near the door facilitates faster, safer unlacing. Try using a tray or stand made of metal or rubber to minimize contact between wet shoes and flooring and speed up air-drying. In a pinch, you can substitute a rag rug, a vinyl place mat, or even an unfolded newspaper. Dedicate a nearby drawer or shelf to a caddy of cleanup tools such as paper towels, disposable wipes, and washcloths.

1. CRATE DEMAND

Gather wet boots and umbrellas in one section of a partitioned wooden crate. Leave other compartments for the morning paper, sports equipment, or pet toys.

2. WASHED UP

A small shower station is the perfect place to rinse dirty shoes and garden tools or give the family dog a bath. A resin fold-down bench provides a comfortable spot to take off mucky footwear or rest a stack of towels.

3. DRIP ZONE

Keep floors and wooden shelving in tip-top shape by placing boots on plastic trays with baking rack inserts.

4. SURFACE MATTER

Pullout shelves outfitted with rubber mats prevent wet shoes from sliding and damaging floors. A drawer with expandable dividers reserves a place for umbrellas.

5. FEEDING TIME

Outdoor fabric on this entry bench cushion shrugs off drips from wet raincoats. Bins below and a wall-mount storage tower hold accessories for kids and pets alike. A waterproof mat stops the dog's water bowl from damaging the floor.

before & after

A busy couple calms their entry while staying realistic about the clutter of living.

BEFORE
problems

Bethany and Ryan wanted an organized entry in their new house, but a new baby and several home improvement projects took precedence over the space. Although the couple purchased a console table and a set of hooks, they lacked a system to manage the space. The room became a jumbled drop zone for shoes, shopping returns, tools, and scrapbooking supplies, much of which spilled over into the couple's living room.

solutions

Expert organizer Donna Smallin Kuper worked with Bethany and Ryan to decide which items needed to stay in the entry, then created permanent homes for those things. "We discovered that the majority of stuff didn't need to be there," Bethany says. "Sorting made us think about what we needed to grab on our way out the door."

1 Labeled metal key tags keep Bethany's and Ryan's keys off the console table.

2 A charging station corrals phones and music devices by the door. A notebook and a cup of pens stand by for quick list making.

3 Shallow bins are replaced by two large wicker baskets, which hold in-season footwear and outgoing library books or store returns.

4 Metal mesh trays in various sizes tame the interior of the console table drawers.

before & after

A front hall closet refines its responsibilities to better serve guests and facilitate entertaining.

BEFORE
problems

Jennifer, Rich, and their two children had other closets off the garage dedicated to their personal gear, so why was the traditional coat closet in the foyer such a mess? The closet's single rod and wire shelf encouraged them to pack the space with rarely worn outerwear, while games, entertaining accessories, and linens ended up in piles on the floor.

AFTER
solutions

With a daughter in college and a son soon to leave for school, Jennifer and Rich's storage needs are changing. Professional organizer Lorie Marrero guided the couple through the process of sorting and prioritizing items. Marrero then upgraded the closet system to Elfa components that better accommodate the items they still want to store in the closet.

1 An open, counter-like shelf on top of four new drawers is a convenient drop spot for spare change and keys.

2 Plastic liners keep wire shelves from leaving imprints on tablecloths and other soft items.

3 Wire baskets make the most of the closet's angled wall. This once-awkward area now holds table leaves and seasonal items used in the nearby dining room.

4 Labels are hidden atop the metal mesh drawers to minimize distractions while reinforcing the new organizing plan.

get going now

Create an effective, attractive drop zone
with quick projects for any size entry.

1 Convert a dining
buffet into an
entry console by
filling a drawer
compartment with
a metal divider to
stand up notebooks
and outgoing mail.

2 Make a custom mail
station by labeling
cubbies with family
member names or
with action words.

3 Hang a utensil tray
on the wall and add
magnetic hooks to
create compart-
ments for keys,
glasses, and notes.

4 Rest a wall cabinet
on its side and top
with a cushion
to fashion a slim
entry bench
with hideaway
capabilities. Add
a short length of
chain to stop the
door from crashing
onto the floor.

ERIN   SIGN   MOM

MOLLY   SEND   DAD

NATE   OFFICE

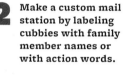

"Get things off the ground with vertical storage solutions. The more floor space, the better in entry areas."

—Donna Smallin Kuper, professional organizer

5 Prevent moisture from ruining floors by keeping wet shoes in a plastic tray lined with decorative pebbles, which allow water to drain to the container's bottom.

6 Attach adhesive letters to charging stations to dedicate spots to specific devices or family members.

7 Fill mini drawers stacked near the door with important (but occasionally used) papers, such as gift certificates, coupons, and school forms.

8 Position a pair of waist-high bookcases at the front of a niche. Stash errant shoes and bags in the newly created mini mudroom.

kitchens

Efficient kitchens provide targeted storage for cooking, cleaning, and entertaining. Get ready to make use of every inch in the heart of your home.

Begin to create a hardworking kitchen by answering three key questions. **Who uses your kitchen?** A kitchen for a growing family has different needs than one for a single chef. Kids need supplies stored at their level and in containers that are super-easy to access; aspiring foodies may want to show off their best tools. **How do you cook?** Home cooks approach meal prep in myriad ways. Give priority space to any tool you use at least once a week; everything else can go in less-accessible spots. **How much food do you truly need to store?** Store only ingredients you'll use in the next month. Plan to purchase the rest during your regular shopping trips.

ultimate kitchen

Food, family, and fun come together in this kitchen that blends open shelving and clever cabinet inserts.

A WORK ISLAND, created by placing a basic dresser and a console table back-to-back, offers storage for multiple needs and serves as a meal preparation spot.

batteries & bulbs

coupons

sweets

coasters & coozies

stamps & stencils

gift bags

Assign a specific function to each drawer or kitchen cabinet.

Island drawer labels *above right* were printed on scrapbook papers and cut to fit the drawers' small glass windows.

A wall-mount bar *above, far right* uses S hooks to keep favorite utensils within easy reach of the cook.

Plastic drawer inserts *right* stop spice jars from rolling around. Labels printed on decorative tape make favorite flavors easy to find.

A pair of curtain panels *far right* mask the open area between upper and base cabinets, serving as a budget-friendly small-appliance garage.

Dish dollies *below right* come in various sizes to stabilize stacks of bowls and plates inside large drawers. Handles allow you to bring items straight to the table at mealtime.

Drawer dividers *below, far right* adjust to span the compartment's length or width and keep small items in check.

save time

Store spare cleaning supplies such as sponges, scrubbers, and cloths in clear plastic shoe drawers—one drawer for each type of item. That way, you can tell at a glance when you're running low.

A slim console table *opposite* backs up to a 12-drawer dresser, supplementing hideaway storage with open areas for frequently used tools and ingredients.

Four plastic tubs *above* fit into a wire cabinet insert to sort recyclables. Large vinyl stickers herald the right spots for glass, paper, cans, and more.

Vinyl shelf liner *right* applied to the console table shelves steadies items.

Undersink organizers *far right* do the dirty work. A piece of painted pegboard puts the inside of the door to work. Cleaners slide out in a high-lipped bin, and reusable plastic bags are corralled in a bin.

in the zone

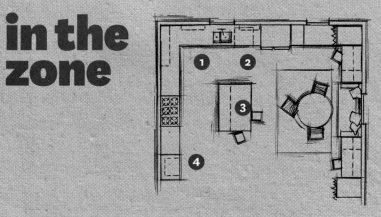

1 Base cabinets with efficient drawers house hardworking items, while open storage presents the pretty stuff.

2 A sink paired with a dishwasher speeds cleanup. Bins in the sink cabinet organize cleaning supplies.

3 The island serves both sides of the kitchen. The large surface is ideal for food prep or homework projects.

4 Recycling bins in a base unit gather empties near the entrance to the garage.

small-space kitchen

Savvy remodeling lets this 10×13-foot kitchen serve up more usable space without expanding one square inch.

A MIX OF DRAWERS, cabinets, and corner units wraps around the corner of this kitchen, efficiently containing culinary necessities. A matching wood front masks a dishwasher to the left of the sink, creating the illusion of more cabinetry.

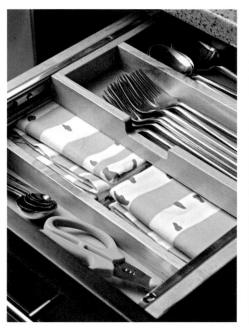

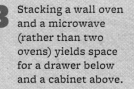

A three-shelf spice rack *above left* **attached inside an upper cabinet door puts flavor enhancers and tea tins within easy reach. Square glass canisters with airtight lids keep tea and coffee fresh while using space more efficiently than round containers.**

A sliding wood tray *above center* **in a drawer adds a bonus layer of storage. Eating utensils reside on the upper level, while less frequently used linens stack below. Soft-close hinges on the drawer help everything stay in place.**

Wire inserts *above right* **in the cabinet above the wall oven position bakeware and cutting boards upright. Fabric-covered storage boxes help less-used items remain clean and grouped by function.**

save space

Tap into a cabinet's toe-kick. Although this area between the floor and cabinet box is typically only 4 to 8 inches tall, you can outfit it with a single, shallow drawer that's perfect for linens or serving platters.

small smarts

1 A slim cabinet in the adjacent dining room holds after-school snacks and seldom-used party supplies.

2 Lazy Susans in base cabinets optimize often-wasted corner space and make pots and pans accessible.

3 Stacking a wall oven and a microwave (rather than two ovens) yields space for a drawer below and a cabinet above.

4 A downdraft cooktop eliminates the need for a bulky exhaust hood.

essential elements | cabinets

Cabinetry is the cornerstone of kitchen storage. No matter your budget, add-ons afford you the following organizing opportunities.

OUT-OF-SIGHT STORAGE

Some culinary essentials just aren't meant to be seen! Doors and drawers unify the look of your kitchen and minimize visual clutter. "Countertop real estate is a hot commodity and should be reserved for items used frequently, if not daily," says organizing expert Stacey Platt. Evaluate how often you use items, then relegate most appliances to inside cabinets and tuck those specialty gadgets into drawers.

OPEN STORAGE

Anything you store in cubbies, racks, or open shelving should be either frequently used or attractive. Possible candidates worthy of display include your everyday dishes, glassware, your main cooking utensils, fresh produce, and serving pieces. Give your displays a sense of order by incorporating risers, miniature shelves, and stands. If you're interested in test-driving open storage in your kitchen, try removing one section of cabinet doors to create a go-to spot for your daily dishes.

"Remember that most cabinet shelves are adjustable. You can also have an additional shelf cut for you if you need more space."

—Laura Leist, professional organizer

DRAWERS

Never underestimate the power of a well-organized drawer. Eliminate jumble by installing a dish or storage system on the bottom of the drawer—or drop in utensil trays and adjustable dividers. Whatever you choose, be ruthless about editing down the items to be stored in your drawers. Getting rid of redundant tools, linens, and other supplies ensures you can shut the drawer after each and every use.

BASE UNIT INTERIORS

Most lower cabinets are voluminous but unstructured. Address depth issues by installing sliding racks or trays that attach to the floor of the cabinet. Whether you choose a slider made of wood, metal, or plastic, you can find a solution that fits your budget and lets you pull the cabinet's contents toward you and out of the dark. Subdivide tall cabinet boxes by building in an additional shelf or standing a wire or wood platform on an existing surface.

essential elements | islands

Add a workstation and watch your meal-prep efficiency grow. Select the version that suits your space, budget, and lifestyle.

ROLLING CART

Choosing a workstation with wheels—or adding wheels to a waist-high table or cabinet you already have—lets you pull your island to center stage when you need it for meal preparation and then push it against a wall or into another room when you need floor space. Be sure your cart has rubber-rimmed casters that can support the island's weight; at least two of the casters should lock so you can safely chop and mix without your work surface wandering away.

WORKTABLE

Transform a sturdy table into a workstation by giving it a tough topper of wood, stainless steel, natural stone, or solid-surfacing. Since the area below the work surface is open, the finished island feels less massive and more casual than a traditional cluster of cabinet boxes. The most effective worktables include a low, heavy-duty shelf for large bowls and bulky appliances. Racks and hooks affixed to the legs and the underside of the countertop give function to the space below.

Use masking tape to mark your island's ideal size and shape first, then buy or have it built to your specifications.

AN ISLAND WITH SPACE FOR EATING

Being able to pull a few stools near your workstation can compensate for a kitchen's lack of dining space. (It's also a great spot for guests to relax or children to do homework.) Starting with a sturdy cabinet base, extend the countertop approximately 12 inches on one or more sides and add appropriate bracing. If floor space is at a premium, mount the extra countertop to the side of a cabinet with piano hinges and flip up the surface when you need it.

MULTIFUNCTIONAL WORKSTATION

Make your island the hub of your cooking space by incorporating electricity and plumbing in well-planned cabinetry. Position cook-centric features such as a sink or cooktop where most needed first, then line the perimeter with features everyone else can enjoy, such as a microwave, a television, a bookcase, or drawers for warming or cooling. To ensure adequate clearance for every feature, plan to work with a kitchen designer or cabinetmaker.

essential elements | pantries

Streamline your shopping and speed up your meal prep with space organized for how you truly cook.

A DEDICATED CABINET

Even if your kitchen doesn't have an "official" pantry, you can designate a cabinet (or several cabinets) as your pantry. Put your most frequently accessed items (breakfast essentials, snacks, oils and vinegars) in an easy-to-access, eye-level spot; relegate canned goods, baking supplies, and other less-frequently used items to lower or higher compartments. Group like items in bins and rely on wood or wire stands to squeeze in an extra layer of storage.

A STAND-ALONE RACK

A shelf, bookcase, or other freestanding unit is an easy pantry substitute. Tuck it into a sliver of space between appliances or position it at the end of a run of cabinets. Install anti-tipping hardware to any unit taller than 36 inches even if your home doesn't include small children. Use trays, bins, and baskets to categorize supplies and keep them from slipping through open shelves. And don't forget to dust your pantry contents as part of your regular cleaning routine.

A SPECIALTY CABINET

Seek out semicustom or custom cabinets with pantry accessories. (See Section Three for the nitty-gritty on installing after-market inserts to existing cupboards.) Look for carousel-style racks and slim pullouts that give you more ways to access canned and boxed items. Given their price tag and permanence, try out specialty cabinets at a home center or showroom before committing. Imagine stocking and retrieving items to see whether the storage features make sense for you.

A WALK-IN PANTRY

A closet or small room dedicated to storing edibles and culinary essentials may seem like a foolproof answer to all your kitchen chaos, but generous spaces require the same planning and organizing strategies as a single cupboard. Get rid of everything that's expired or you don't use. Group similar items together, placing stuff you use frequently between waist and eye level. Allow yourself some open space to hold the occasional influx of party or seasonal supplies.

challenges | culinary tools

The latest gadgets and gizmos are great, but for stress-free meal preparation, you have to be able to find the right tool instantly.

However you choose to store small appliances and cooking utensils, moderation is key. Edit down the contents of a countertop crock to just the tools you've used in the past week. Allow only one layer of utensils in a drawer; expandable dividers and trays can help you divvy up available space based on function and frequency of use. Store small appliances just one item deep on shelves, and use baskets or plastic zippered bags to isolate accessories for each appliance.

Before you stash a tool in a prominent spot, consider if you've used it in the past six months. If not, it may be time to donate it.

1. GREAT GROUPS

Sort utensils by tasks, such as stirring, flipping, cutting, and barbecuing. Built-in or spring-loaded dividers create distinct segments in a drawer.

2. BIG BOX CONCEPT

The tambour door on this corner appliance garage is placed in line with the wall—rather than on an awkward diagonal—so items don't get lost in the back.

3. CENTER STAGE

Place an appliance you use daily—such as a coffeemaker or microwave—on a waist-height shelf inside a large cabinet. Install a dedicated outlet and partner the appliance with pertinent accessories.

4. TIGHT SQUEEZE

A tall, slim cabinet outfitted with rolling shelves lets you arrange a bevy of tools in a column behind a single door.

5. PERFECT POCKETS

Hang a clear shoe bag inside a pantry door and slip in culinary items. Label each pouch with a vinyl sticker. Cut shoe bags along stitched seams with kitchen scissors to fit in smaller spaces.

challenges | food & spices

Optimize your pantry, fridge, and freezer to efficiently store more edible items and preserve freshness longer.

If you're gonna use it, you gotta see it. Yes, this principle applies to many areas of your home, but it's critical for food storage. Haphazardly stocked food leads to wasted time and money. You forget what you have, purchase duplicates, and end up with even less storage space. Stop the cycle by decanting groceries into clear containers. The process adds a few minutes to unpacking, but you're less likely to wonder if you have enough flour at home during your next shopping trip.

Group like items to simplify prep time, such as a single shelf or bin for baking, stir-frying, roasting, or grilling.

1. LED BY WORDS

Apply cold-resistant adhesive labels to refrigerator and freezer shelves and containers, or loop luggage tags through basket-style containers. Affix a holder with permanent marker to the underside of a shelf to aid in speedy labeling.

2. SLIPPED DETAILS

Clip nutrition info and cooking instructions from original packaging and slip into clear plastic pockets adhered to the outside of storage containers.

3. KEY INGREDIENTS

To prevent pileup of half-empty boxes and bags, shift dry goods to clear plastic containers with airtight lids. Look for suites of containers with standard-size lids and stacking capabilities.

4. STANDING OVATION

Use tiered risers so nothing gets lost in the back of cabinets. Ensure freshness by jotting down the date you opened an item with a marker.

5. LAYERED LOGIC

Place tall containers in the rear so short items in front remain visible. Allocate prime real estate for leftovers in labeled grab-and-go containers.

challenges | corners

Tailor the shelves and cabinets where two kitchen walls meet to pack in smart storage and eye-catching display space.

Corners in most kitchens are structurally necessary and unquestionably challenging. In general, go with a less-is-more approach rather than installing complex (and often expensive) solutions. Focus on storing things just one item deep. Replace deep shelves and cabinets with shallower versions. What you sacrifice in cubic footage, you more than make up for in easier accessibility and better aesthetics.

Cookbooks, serving pieces, and decorative items can make these show-off spots both beautiful and functional.

1. IN THE OPEN
Show off attractive dishware with open L-shape shelves that wrap around a corner. Trim doubles as bracing along the underside of the shelves, eliminating the need for space-hogging supports.

2. TRIPLE PLAY
Installing floating shelves in a corner increases their stability and load-bearing capabilities.

3. BOOK NOOK
Rather than positioning shelves on the diagonal, this tower-like cabinet follows the line of wall cabinets. Nothing on the perpendicular wall blocks access to the cookbooks.

4. DAINTY DISPLAY
Quarter-circle and triangular shelves provide just enough space for collectibles or plants. Clear-yet-strong materials, such as tempered glass or acrylic sheeting, offer order with minimal visual clutter.

5. COUNTER LINK
Countertop corners rarely get used for meal prep, so extend a wall cabinet to the counter to create focal-point storage for large pieces and appliances.

challenges | cleaning & recycling

A spotless, streamlined kitchen is in your future when you simplify your housekeeping and recycling routines.

For a cleaner, greener kitchen, eliminate anything that keeps you from easily picking up a spray bottle and sponge or gathering recyclables. Stash go-to cleaners and tools at the front of a closed cabinet on a tray that catches any drips. Downsize to a small recycling bin and make regular trips to a larger container in your garage. Get familiar with your community's recycling policy. Many areas now recycle plastics with SPI codes 1 through 7 and do not require you to separate items.

save space

Stow just what you need to clean the kitchen under the sink. Combine or toss out half-empty bottles of cleaners. They may still be usable, but there's no point in cluttering up your cabinets with items you've moved on from.

1. SPIN CONTROL
Partitioned lazy-Susan-style bins optimize a deep corner cabinet. Better yet, the bins are located near the stove and sink, so rinsing and sorting items is a cinch.

2. A GREAT DIVIDE
Make sustainability easy by assigning drawers for paper, plastic, and metal recyclables. Line drawers with bags or bins so you can effortlessly lift and transport materials to the recycling bin.

3. DISH DUTY
Stow items like soap, detergent, rags, and sponges in a shallow drawer to minimize counter clutter. Use plastic sock sorters to separate items.

4. HIDE AND SEEK
A pullout near the sink lets you access supplies from either side. Put your grab-and-go items at the top; lesser-used items go on lower shelves.

5. HUNG UP
Hang scrub brushes on small hooks and drape towels on over-the-door bars to encourage air-drying and prevent mold growth. A lazy Susan on a low shelf means all cleaners are just a spin away.

After taking stock of what really belongs in their reach-in pantry, a couple says goodbye to clutter.

BEFORE
problems

A random mix of stuff, from wedding presents to paper party supplies, crowded Samantha and Ben's pantry. The jumble made it hard to see what was on the shelves, resulting in the couple buying more of what they already had—which further amplified the chaos.

"I could never take a good inventory of what I had," Samantha says. "I knew the pantry had to be reorganized, but I didn't know where to start. Thinking about cleaning it was exhausting."

solutions

Professional organizer Laura Leist worked with the couple to devise a plan. Samantha removed every item and sorted those they didn't need into "Trash," "Donate," and "Garage Sale" boxes. She grouped the remaining items by function and took careful measurements of shelves and the space between shelves. Only then did she buy new organizing products.

1 Magazine organizers corral cookbooks. Slender cereal keepers make the most of shelf depth.

2 Canisters that are see-through, stackable, and square fit on the shelves like building blocks. Vacuum-sealing lids are ideal for staples.

3 A plate rack manages baking pans and racks.

4 Erasable labels identify what's in containers whose contents change frequently.

before & after

Changes in a family's storage behaviors make the difference in maintaining this step-in pantry.

BEFORE

problems

With 10 sturdy shelves and a generous footprint, this step-in space should have been sufficient for Susan and her family. Instead, items were stacked willy-nilly, including on the floor and nearby counters. Dry goods mingled with small appliances, and party supplies and paper goods sometimes tumbled from the upper shelves.

"After 12 years of living this way, I figured this was just how the pantry had to be," Susan says.

solutions

Professional organizer Lorie Marrero focused on maintenance strategies, basic containers, and simple labels. "Cool new products are not always the big answer," she says. "Often, it's the behaviors and actions that matter more."

After removing and sorting the contents, Susan stocked the pantry only with food, paper goods, and frequently used appliances. She reserved eye-level shelves for daily items such as cereal and snacks and declared the floor off-limits for food.

1 Labels reinforce the places Susan chose for storing each type of item. Clear canisters hold a working supply of basics, while backstocked items reside behind.

2 Bulk purchases are now opened and stored in labeled containers, which means fewer big boxes filled with unknown quantities.

3 Turntables optimize the deep corners and hold frequently used bottled ingredients.

4 Disposable tableware resides in a single box. Susan can drop in plates, cups, napkins, and other party supplies— yet still see the contents through the clear container.

get going now

Little updates yield major benefits. Each of these mini projects takes only a few minutes to complete.

1 Hang a clipboard inside your pantry door or mount it to the outside of your refrigerator to track what you have and what you need.

2 Put all sandwich- and lunch-making elements in handled containers that transport easily from fridge to counter.

3 Create vertical partitions in a cabinet with pairs of spring-loaded curtain rods to keep baking sheets, platters, cutting boards, and trays in line.

4 Transform a deep drawer into your party supply spot. Line the drawer with paper, then stack cups by size and material. Drop flatware into pencil cups. Use a desktop folder rack to stand paper goods upright.

Can't set aside an afternoon for organizing? Chunk projects into 15-minute blocks and spread them out over a few days.

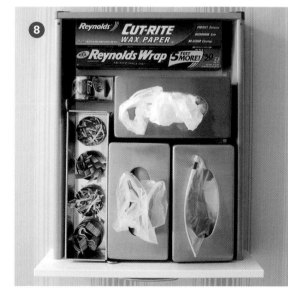

5 Group frequently used oils and spices in a high-lipped tray with handles. Stash the entire container inside a cabinet or on a pullout shelf until it's cooking time.

6 Label the lids of your spice jars and store them in a drawer or basket. Use a desk tray intended for office supplies to stand everything upright.

7 Gather kid-friendly dishes and accessories in a single, easy-to-access cabinet. Use cereal dispensers to portion out cereal and snacks.

8 For faster access, sort plastic bags by type and then stuff into covers designed to hold boxes of facial tissue.

eating spaces

When you pull a chair to the table, you want the chaos of life to fade away. This section shows you how to focus on enjoying food and family without the fuss.

Whether you have an eat-in kitchen or a formal dining room, ask yourself the following. **What do you really do in your eating space?** If you do more than eat there, incorporate solutions that will help you and your family efficiently shift among studying, working, playing, and enjoying meals. **What other rooms connect with your eating space?** How your kitchen, entry, or living room functions likely needs to be in harmony with any changes you make in the eating space. **What's your hosting style?** Entertaining guests or setting an intricate table can be a stress-free endeavor when you create an organized station for dinnerware, linens, and finishing touches.

ultimate dining room

This dining room with built-ins and banquette seating affords ample space for gathering and entertaining, as well as completing paperwork.

A PAIR OF BUILT-INS provide gracious display space for specialty dishes and antique items that would otherwise hide in a buffet or kitchen cabinet.

save space

Instead of using up valuable bedroom or living room space for an office, treat your formal dining area as a double-duty room. Bureaus, drawers, and cabinets can hide supplies when it's time to eat.

Banquette seating *far left* follows the bay window's angles and offers flexible seating for up to eight. The cushions can be removed and the seats lifted to reveal extra storage for seasonal items.

Silver binder clips *left* organize napkin sets by color. Labels help sort linens and other items.

Entertaining supplies *below left,* such as table linens, candles, napkin rings, and vases, stow away on pullout shelves within the built-in's base. Fabric-wrapped cork panels inside the doors are perfect for pinning guest lists or supply inventories.

ultimate dining room

save time

Modular ideas, such as a homework caddy, are great for eating spaces. Take it out for homework, then put it away at mealtime. If a caddy is too small, try a rolling cart that you scoot into a closet or an adjacent room.

A classic sideboard *opposite* houses hosting essentials in the base and provides counter space for everyday items. A drop-down panel and a pullout shelf in the nearby built-in create a mini desk.

The base cabinet *above right* in one built-in hosts a printer, document trays, magazine holders, and office supplies for work sessions.

A charging station *above, far right* ensures phones and other devices are ready to go. The front pockets hold cards, sticky notes, and pens.

Silver and china *below left* stay tucked away inside a sideboard drawer, secured by utensil holders with lined bottoms.

Barware and wine *below, far left* reside on shelves and dividers inside the sideboard. Bartending utensils stowed on a removable tray facilitate quick set-up of a beverage station on the sideboard.

in the zone

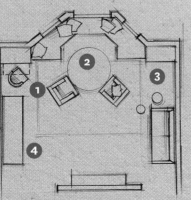

1 A slender built-in with a hidden desk offers enough space for a computer and a calendar to manage daily family life.

2 A bay window makes the dining space feel large, but homey banquette seating maintains a welcoming vibe.

3 A pair of built-ins with open shelving showcase decorative objects and serving pieces in the upper areas and less-lovely necessities in doored compartments below.

4 A generous buffet targets storage for fine dinnerware, utensils, and wine.

small-space dining room

With square footage limited, the owners of this dining room added skinny storage to satisfy kids and welcome guests.

STACKED TOWERS of semicustom cabinets and drawers flank the dining area's French doors, boosting architectural character and giving the look of built-ins without the price tag.

A DIY wine rack
above left **made by
stacking spray-painted
cans inside one
compartment in the left
storage tower puts an
array of vino at the ready.
Barware in trays and
ingredients stand at the
ready on the shelf above.**

A wicker tray
above middle **transports
small plates and
condiments from kitchen
to table. It also aids in
speedy cleanup when
the party ends.**

A low cabinet
above right **facilitates
snack time with clear
containers of goodies and
baskets of plastic
silverware and straws.
Storing everything at kid
height encourages older
kids to help themselves.**

save space

Free up your kitchen cabinets by stashing specific entertaining supplies in the areas where you use them. Try keeping wine and bar napkins in the dining room, bowls in the family room, and snacks in your office.

small smarts

1 A column of semicustom kitchen cabinets holds adult supplies such as barware and wine.

2 French doors to a small patio provide a seamless transition from dinner parties to outdoor entertaining.

3 Filling the low portion of this cabinet with snacks and plastic dishes allows kids to serve themselves.

4 A round table is easier to navigate in a tight room. Guests can pull up an extra chair for meals, homework projects, or game nights.

essential elements

Rediscover the top of your table by surrounding it with supporting storage pieces that look good and function effortlessly.

SERVING STATION

You don't need to invest in a traditional sideboard, but you do need to support your table with a landing area that's at least 10 inches wide and sturdy enough to support food platters, a stack of extra dishes, or an array of beverages. If space is at a premium, set up a pair of TV trays or roll in a kitchen work cart. Make sure the surface is durable and water-resistant; you want to enjoy the meal rather than have to drop everything to clean up spills.

DISH STORAGE

Divide tableware into everyday and special occasion. Your everyday pieces need to be super-simple to see, grab, and restock after cleaning; your special stuff can go in high cabinets or a showy hutch. "Give yourself permission to adjust a cabinet's interior shelves," says professional organizer Lorie Marrero. "They were probably installed symmetrically and consistently years ago. You'll likely be able to store more and access items more easily if you move some shelves closer together." If you can't move the shelves, add helper shelves and risers.

"Undesignated space is the key problem in eating spaces. Rather than dumping stuff on the table, assign specific places for specific items and create destination stations."
—Lorie Marrero, professional organizer

BENCHES AND BANQUETTES

Replace a few dining chairs with a freestanding bench or built-in seat and watch your storage capabilities grow. Lidded seats work well for stashing folded linens, seasonal decor, and serving pieces. Cabinets with doors you can open without lifting the seat or removing cushions are appropriate for items you need every month or so, such as small appliances or board games. Bonus: Benches and banquettes adjust quickly to host more diners—just scoot everyone a little closer.

ORGANIZED ENTERTAINING

Do you really entertain, or do you just dream about it? Whatever your answer, you can probably edit down to only serving pieces, linens, specialty dinnerware, and tabletop flourishes you've used in the past year. If possible, move your entertaining gear out of the kitchen, which should be home first and foremost to daily-use items. If you're struggling with Grandma's china (and it is OK to let go of it), Marrero recommends displaying it or putting it in safe long-term storage.

challenges | setting the table

Having the right dishes, napkins, and silverware ready makes setting a beautiful table simple. Try these hosting tricks today.

A china hutch filled with tableware may be gorgeous to behold, but it's probably not a great everyday solution. Show off your finest, but position the dishes and silverware you use daily in a spot that's convenient for both setting the table and scrubbing at the sink or dishwasher. Get young family members involved in pre- and post-meal duties by storing durable ceramic or melamine dinnerware in a base cabinet or drawer outfitted with stabilizing racks or pegs.

Sort dishes by use. Everyday plates should be reachable without a stepladder; special-occasion dinnerware can be stored in harder-to-reach places.

1. TRIPLE PLAY
Use drawer dividers to sort decorative items by type. Here, three styles of candles are separated for easy retrieval.

2. LITTLE EXTRAS
Place salt and pepper shakers, napkin rings, and tealights in the divided sections of a storage caddy designed for teacups. A small list taped inside the cabinet door gives a quick reminder of contents.

3. TOP SHELF
An undershelf organizer hangs in a pantry, creating a spot for neatly folded napkins.

4. ON DISPLAY
Skip the wooden china hutch and show off dishware on a wrought-iron baker's rack or plant stand. Designed to support the weight of stand mixers and potted plants, these pieces are sturdy enough to show off platters, pitchers, and stacks of plates.

5. BASKET CASE
Make extra tableware part of your decor by stacking plates and linens in an open cubby or bookcase. A few baskets manage small items and conveniently travel to the table when needed.

challenges | entertaining

Whether you're throwing a cocktail party or hosting last-minute dinner guests, strive for effortless entertaining.

The faster you can get the good times rolling, the better, so collect your go-to hosting supplies in one location and plan to add perishable and hot or cold edibles when guests arrive. Skip last-minute stress by removing excess packaging on paper goods, beverages, and snacks.

Buffets and serving carts are conventional choices, but don't overlook the potential of an end table, repurposed media armoire, or handled crate as your good-time destination.

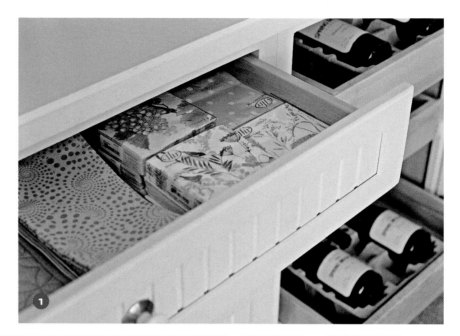

1. DRAWER POWER
Shallow drawers can handle linens stacked by size or shape, as well as wine bottles stabilized by cut-down egg cartons.

2. SNACK CENTRAL
Unpack treats as soon as you get home from the supermarket. Store in airtight canisters or divide into snack-size portions in plastic bags.

3. HIDE AND SEEK
Curtains on a side table conceal entertaining necessities below. Loops on the bottom edge hook to buttons near the tabletop, clearing access to party essentials while setting up the buffet.

4. MIX IT UP
Combine soda, drink mixes, and tonic water in a large bin. On the day of your event, chill the entire container or set items into an ice bucket. Encourage guests to help themselves to cool libations.

5. MOBILE PARTY
Refinish a tea cart and stock with indoor/outdoor amenities, such as napkins and bamboo plates. Add a drink carafe and a bowl of snacks for a go-anywhere fun spot.

get going now

Bring breakfast, lunch, or dinner to the table more quickly with a few simple adjustments.

1 Retool a rolling kitchen island as a party cart. Add wire baskets for snacks and hooks for hand towels. Drop utensils in a small bucket and stack extra plastic dishware casually on a low shelf.

2 Dedicate a corner of your kitchen or dining room to a breakfast zone. A wire shelf holds bread, oats, and coffee. S hooks dangle mugs, and dispensers keep cereal at the ready.

3 Mount 1x3 trim to the wall as shallow plate racks for your prettiest platters and trays.

4 Hang a trio of tower-style bookcases sideways for a wall's worth of entertaining. Wider spacing between the top and middle units creates a serving ledge; baskets on the lowest level hold less-attractive essentials.

Split a large organizing project into two or three small tasks that you can complete in 20-minute segments.

5 Low on dining room storage space? Store entertaining supplies elsewhere in a large lidded basket. Handles make carrying this kit from room to room easier.

6 Expand the duties of a wine rack by filling the slots with other bottled drinks, rolled napkins, and tapers. Tack your favorite drink and appetizer recipes to corkboard affixed inside a cabinet door.

7 Increase storage capabilities inside cabinets or below shelves by installing a wire rack for hanging stemware.

8 Convert a mail sorter into a caddy for casual entertaining that's always ready to go. Stock with plates, napkins, and cutlery. Or use the caddy to gather favorite dry nibbles or breakfast goodies.

living spaces

Whether you call them living, family, or media rooms, these areas are where people and their stuff gather. Here's how to get smart about sharing space.

Balance personal needs and public spaces by pondering the following. **How do you really use the space?** Today's gathering spaces must allow for enjoying media and gaming, as well as conversing, relaxing, and reading. Be honest about what activities you do together so you can pick the best storage pieces and furniture. **What needs to go?** Media habits and electronics have changed radically in the past decade. Give yourself permission to replace that classic entertainment center. **What rules are you willing to establish?** You don't need to become a dictator, but keeping a family room tidy requires setting clear expectations and enforcing them firmly and consistently.

ultimate living room

This large, eclectic living space accommodates the needs of a family with young boys thanks to several functional zones.

A canvas basket *above left* rounds up controllers and other gaming accessories. No lid means one fewer barrier to putting things away at the end of a session.

A two-tier sofa table *left* displays stacks of favorite novels. Matching baskets below hold blankets and magazines.

A quartet of cubes *below* can form a single central coffee table—or each piece can easily move to become a side table, a footstool, or impromptu seating for guests. The backless sofa on the left encourages connection with the study zone beyond.

A FLAT-PANEL TV modernizes the family hearth. Identical freestanding cabinets on either side of the fireplace feel like built-ins and are filled with media, games, and other fun-time essentials.

ultimate living room

save time
Putting desk supplies in clear plastic or acrylic boxes makes it easy for kids to spot exactly what they need while studying or working on projects. And with contents on display, you don't need labels to tell you what belongs where.

Clear acrylic chairs *opposite* take up less visual space than bulky office chairs, allowing other furniture and accessories to shine. Console tables and table lamps are stylish stand-ins for traditional desks and reading lamps.

A media-centric cabinet *above right* conceals CDs, DVDs, video players, and gaming consoles. Doors with frosted-glass panels shift the focus to art displayed on top.

Clear media cases *above far right* organize entertainment neatly and slide into nearby cabinets.

Slide-out plastic bins *right* hold pens, paper clips, and sticky notes for kids studying in the adjacent work space.

The homework cabinet *far right* hosts a wireless printer, office supplies, and letter trays labeled for each family member.

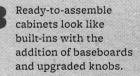

in the zone

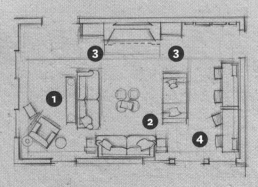

1 A comfy armchair and a console table filled with reading material become a cozy reading corner for Mom or Dad.

2 Arranged in a U shape, three couches allow for socializing, gaming, and movie-watching.

3 Ready-to-assemble cabinets look like built-ins with the addition of baseboards and upgraded knobs.

4 A work space along the far wall connects parents and kids. Two long, narrow desks comfortably fit four.

small-space living room

A mix of stylish containers brings beautiful function to classic built-ins in this pint-size gathering space.

BUILT-IN SHELVES to the left of the fireplace are filled with bins of toys, arts and crafts supplies, and family games; the shelves on the right hold parents' things. The cabinets' tops blend with the mantel for displaying favorite art and collectibles.

A medley of containers *above left,* including wire baskets, hatboxes, and ribbon-embellished bins, keep parents' reading materials and hobby supplies orderly and accessible in one set of the room's built-in cabinets.

A shapely console table *above center* perched at the edge of the room works as a drop zone that stops personal odds and ends from migrating into the shared gathering space beyond. A woven tray catches daily mail and pocket contents.

Handled baskets *above right* are assigned to family members, giving each a role in the task of picking up the room at the end of each day. The baskets also travel efficiently to other rooms and work spaces when needed.

save space

Limited floor space requires that your ottomans and occasional tables do double or triple duty. The footstool in this room functions as a coffee table; the top flips opens to reveal a spot for blankets or board games.

small smarts

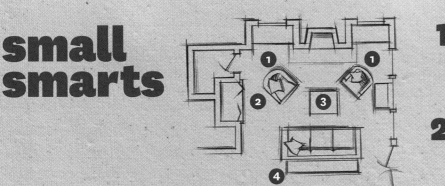

1 Built-in shelves with glass-panel doors complete the focal-point fireplace while keeping the family's favorite activities close at hand.

2 A media center quietly blends in with the room's other cabinetry, facilitating a movie night or friendly gaming competition.

3 Functional furniture in the seating area creates a relaxing vibe while stashing amenities such as throws and pillows.

4 A sofa-hugging table outfitted with a tray and baskets turns an underused stretch of space into a purposeful drop zone.

essential elements

After you know what you want
from your living room, you're ready
to select furniture and containers
that meet your expectations.

BUILT-INS & BOOKCASES
Sturdy shelving is the best investment you can make to bring order to
a living room. Whether you choose a freestanding case or have a unit
built in, look for hardwood frames and shelves with metal brackets
that are easy to reposition as your storage needs change. "The best
bookcases combine open shelving and closed compartments,"
professional organizer Kathy Jenkins says. "Because no matter how
organized your life is, you don't need or want to see everything."

ELECTRONICS & MEDIA
Before flat-panel TVs, compact components, and digital storage,
managing your media meant purchasing a huge entertainment center.
"A better strategy nowadays is to spread storage duties throughout
the room, storing DVDs, gaming, and other items in smaller pieces
with specifically assigned duties," Jenkins says. Start with shallow
cases for the areas below and on either side of your television. Strive
for good-looking, symmetrically placed solutions because you're much
more likely to keep up with a system that's aesthetically pleasing.

"Living rooms often evolve unconsciously: You have a child. You purchase a gaming system. Take time to consciously stop yourself and ask what you really want the room to be."

—**Kathy Jenkins,** professional organizer

OCCASIONAL TABLES

The best side, console, and coffee tables do more than merely look good; they work hard as spots to rest your feet, have a seat, or stash stuff. Resting an attractive tray or caddy on top of a table instantly ups its usefulness. Fill the new container with reading material, favorite entertainment options, or snacks. Calm any concerns about marring a table's top by having a piece of glass or clear acrylic cut to size.

PERSONAL STUFF

Don't let kid toys, teen gear, or adult work projects take over a shared room. Carve out a small, specific spot within a gathering space for each family member. Your solution might be several labeled baskets, designated shelves, or assigned cubbies. Jenkins recommends setting a simple guideline. Example: "At the end of the day, all your stuff goes back in your bin, and your bin goes back to your room, the playroom, or a specific bookcase because that's were it belongs in our home."

challenges | media

Sort and stow your family's music, video, and gaming supplies with solutions that flex as technologies change.

Yes, streaming media is the way of the future, but DVDs and CDs linger, and gaming systems seem to proliferate. Gather all your media and determine what entertainment options you enjoy most. Dedicate prime space for these items and store the rest in bins, boxes, or binders in a nearby closet or built-in. "If you're not willing to archive some media or pack away a less-used game system," Kathy Jenkins says, "ask yourself what you are willing to give up instead. A chair? An end table? You have to get tough with other aspects of a room if you can't let go."

Put your media on a diet by replacing bulky plastic and cardboard packaging with protective vinyl sleeves.

1. QUICK CHANGE
Rest gaming elements on a tray that pulls out when it's time for some friendly competition.

2. FILED AWAY
Free up shelf space by sorting music or movie discs by genre, sliding them into plastic pages with pockets, and filing them in labeled binders.

3. WALL HUGGER
Shallow shelves and cabinets are ideal for organizing media, books, and flat-panel TVs. Work with bookcases and console cabinetry to achieve a piece that's shallow yet serviceable.

4. DOUBLE DUTY
Large video game accessories fill an ottoman outfitted with safety hinges. Trays inside the compartment minimize cord tangles.

5. PATTERN PLAY
Slide an open shelf unit under a wall-mount TV and fill with a mix of colorfully coordinated boxes and bins for housing movies and photos. Adhesive labels on lids are unobtrusive reminders of what goes where.

challenges | collections

Present your passions and personality in an orderly fashion with these savvy strategies for showing off favorite things.

Think like a museum curator as you stock shelves with collectibles. Your goal is to display your very best items now while also allowing yourself 20 percent room for growth.

Keep your collections interesting—for guests and yourself—by rotating in two or three new items every month or season. Put the removed items into long-term storage in labeled containers so you know where to find them later.

Focus on class rather than mass by displaying only a dozen or fewer of your most favorite collectibles at one time.

1. FRAMED FINESSE

Create a gallery-style wall that's easy to update by combining shelves and hung artwork. Hang two shelves next to each other to give the illusion of a long horizontal display ledge.

2. SECOND LIFE

Refinished dresser drawers hung side-by-side serve as a modular display system for vases and other shapely items. A board shelf connects and unifies mismatched pieces.

3. CLASSIC CACHE

Coffee-table books, lamps, and urns arranged like a cityscape on a side table encourage the eye to linger and explore a mix of special objects. A glass apothecary jar holds stones from travels.

4. TINY TREASURES

Mount boxes lined with scraps of decorative paper to the wall using picture hooks. Arrange keepsakes inside and atop for a display that's multidimensional.

5. TALL ORDER

Extend shelving to the ceiling to show off collections. Place favorite books and frequently used items at eye level or below. Be sure to secure shelves that are more than 5 feet tall to the wall.

before & after

Chaotic bookcases find calm without sacrificing the fun stuff that brings a family together.

BEFORE
problems

When they moved into their new home, Molly and Kurt were thrilled with the wall of handsome built-ins in the living room. They soon realized that the four sections of shelving were almost too much of a good thing. "Some sections looked cluttered, some looked empty, and some just looked ugly," Molly says of the wide-open spaces filled with CDs, DVDs, electronic components, and mementos.

solutions

Accepting that electronic components and cords are never going to be beautiful, Molly worked with a carpenter to add two sets of doors with reeded glass inserts to the built-in's center sections. In the side designated for media, Molly introduced a bevy of small upgrades that yield major impact.

1 Wire racks hold stemware, and wicker trays collect tumblers and beverages on the top shelf. DVDs are sorted by genre in scrapbooking-supply boxes and binders, while a lap desk helps cool the computer Molly uses to stream videos. The retractable bottom shelf boosts access to components.

2 Circular cuts in the built-in's top and sidewalls help untangle cables. Ties and plastic sleeves further streamline cords.

3 A bamboo silverware holder transforms into a caddy for cords and gaming accessories.

4 A strip of hook-and-loop tape affixed inside one of the cabinets secures remotes. "Everyone's pretty good about putting back remotes at the end of the day," Molly says.

get going now

Make several of these little adjustments to ensure your gathering spaces look tidy and meet the needs of everyone in your family.

1 Fill coffee table drawers with favorite board games. Stash card games along with extra pens, paper pads, and dice within shallow desk drawer organizers.

2 Slip a bench or open-back bookcase between chairs to squeeze in a place to set drinks, remote controls, or magazines.

3 A silverware caddy steps out of the kitchen to deftly collect remotes, eyeglasses, writing supplies, or snacks.

4 Create a "lost and found" bin for each family member using clear acrylic magazine holders and vinyl adhesive letters. Drop items left around the house into the bins throughout the day, then make it a habit for the whole family to empty their bins nightly.

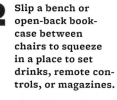

For public spaces, choose furniture and containers that stand up to daily use by multiple family members.

5 Deposit similar items in glass vases and jars. Not only will you better manage life's ephemera, you'll end up with quirky art pieces.

6 Attach metal mesh bins to the side of a media cabinet to hold chargers, gaming components, and stray discs.

7 Glide a serving tray under upholstered seating to establish a hideaway spot for magazines and newspapers.

8 Stand board games and puzzles on their sides inside a cabinet with the aid of a rubber-coated wire pan rack.

bathrooms

Keeping your home's most personal spaces tidy begins with smart organization and durable (yet beautiful) solutions that stand up to daily use.

Regardless of size or amenities, baths look and function better when you answer the following questions. **Who uses the room?** Time to get real! Every item you store in a bath must cater to the specific needs of the person or people who use it. **How can you combine cleaning and organizing?** A clean bath feels more organized, so work to simplify the items you keep and display. Also, every surface should be easy to rinse or wipe, and every container should be dishwasher-safe. **What secondary spaces can you use?** Store essentials in the bath proper, but look to nearby closets, cabinets, and bedrooms as alternative spots to stash extra toiletries and linens.

ultimate bathroom

Spa-inspired accessories and
inexpensive add-ons soothe this
streamlined master bathroom.

wrap   relax   pamper

A SLEEK BENCH
built into a niche outside
the shower is an inviting
place to apply lotion,
paint nails, or put on
shoes. A heated towel bar
encourages pampering.

Practical systems for managing shower necessities, towels, and cleaning supplies bring order to morning routines.

Leather-clad trays
top keep bracelets and necklaces tangle-free. Acrylic organizers in the drawer below sort cosmetics and are a cinch to clean.

A hair-care caddy
right is secured inside a vanity door with suction cups. A hair dryer and other tools plug in to the cabinet's built-in outlet.

Retractable towel bars
far right within a cabinet save space and swivel to layer hand towels and washcloths.

A pullout shelf
below right added under the sink holds extra mouthwash and soap. Less-used items, such as hydrogen peroxide and replacement razors, reside further back.

Stacking containers
below, far right separate sponges and small cleaners from taller spray bottles.

PAPER PRODUCTS

TRAVEL TOILETRIES

WASH CLOTHS & HAND TOWELS

BATH TOWELS

save money
Although this bath sports custom cabinets and luxury details, all the organizing inserts and accessories came from home centers and discount retailers. Installation required only a cordless drill and basic hand tools.

A built-in armoire
left holds towels, washcloths, and extra paper goods. Labels on shelves and storage boxes make staying organized second nature.

Spa supplies
above stay safe in a set of teak baskets that reside underneath the bath bench. Embroidered labels indicate contents.

Adjustable dividers
right arrange delicates in a bathroom drawer for easier dressing.

Self-adhesive letters
far right applied inside drawers mark contents discreetly. You can inexpensively customize your look by varying fonts, colors, and sizes.

in the zone

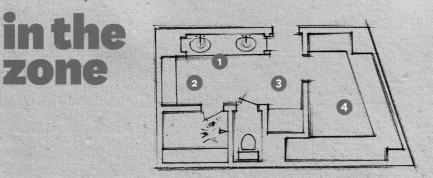

1 Grooming is swift with a mix of shallow drawer organizers and slide-out shelves in the lower compartments.

2 A bench is ideal for toweling off or indulging in spa treatments.

3 The upper portion of this recessed built-in functions as a linen closet, while a lower drawer holds clothing.

4 An adjacent walk-in closet carves out space for sorting laundry, getting dressed, and prepping for trips.

small-space bathroom

A petite bath makes the most of every inch with smart cabinetry and right-scale extras.

MIRRORED INSERTS on cabinet doors and drawers make this tiny, windowless room feel brighter and larger.

A cushioned bench *above left* **packs a storage punch thanks to a low drawer for extra towels, shampoo, and shower gel. Terry cloth upholstery provides a place to dry off right outside the shower.**

An angled cabinet *above center* **designed to tuck under the eaves serves as a medicine cabinet over the toilet. Brushes, cosmetics, and hair-care tools live in the drawer below.**

Undersink cabinets *above right* **hold hand towels, paper products, and cleaning supplies. Surrounding drawers hold grooming supplies and makeup.**

save space

Shelving recessed under eaves and into the space between studs boosts the capacity of small rooms. In this bath, cubbies are just large enough to hold baskets and stacks of washcloths.

small smarts

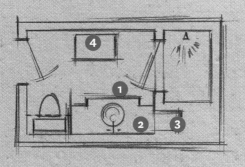

1 A vessel sink allows for more space in the cabinet below, while a bumped-out center vanity adds extra cubic inches.

2 Decorative containers on the vanity hold daily-use supplies such as cotton balls.

3 Recessed shelving, situated in a gap between wall studs, adds extra space-saving opportunities.

4 A bench outside the shower offers freestanding, movable storage for bath necessities.

ultimate linen closet

This well-stocked closet houses linens, laundry, and toiletries with high-functioning style.

Metal wine racks *opposite* **are perfectly partitioned for rolled linens. A large bucket holds extra toilet paper.**

A rolling hamper *above, far left* **with embroidered bags facilitates sorting. Soiled garments are easy to treat with a stain pen tied to the system.**

An acrylic caddy *far left* **holds nail polish, files, and remover for manicure sessions. A nearby bin of cleaning supplies can be removed when it's time to tidy up. The shelves are wrapped in durable oilcloth.**

Cooking oil flasks *left* **and other acrylic kitchen canisters decant soap, bubble bath, salts, and other sundries. A lazy Susan puts everything at your fingertips with an effortless spin. Adhesive letters identify contents.**

Store items with similar functions in caddies or buckets for easy portability.

in the zone

1 Hooks inside closet doors provide places to hang wet towels and buckets for each family member's toiletries.

2 A divided hamper slides below closet shelves and hides dirty laundry.

3 A lazy Susan lined with a scrap of nonslip oilcloth rotates to ensure smaller items don't get lost.

4 Repurposed wine caddies store about two weeks' worth of rolled towels.

essential elements | sinks

A beautifully functioning bath begins with a well-organized vanity. Here's how to optimize yours regardless of style or size.

PEDESTAL

Sculptural sinks require supporting storage pieces. To maximize this type of wash station, stand in front of it and look in all directions, including the floor around the pedestal, the ceiling above, and the wall that supports the mirror. Install wall shelves around the vanity area or position tower-style cabinets nearby. Add hooks to any sliver of space wider than 6 inches. Give each hook a specific duty, such as holding towels, robes, clothes, or buckets or bags for personal supplies.

OPEN CONSOLE

Think strategically about the items you place in the airy area under this type of sink. Work with the curve of the plumbing, storing a combination of tall and short items. Add shallow baskets or trays to stabilize tall bottles and stacks of frequently used linens. Store only items that can stand up to splashing water and dripping toiletries. Keep the undersink area fresh and appealing by wiping, dusting, or vacuuming there during your cleaning routine.

Reserve open storage for daily-use items. Closed storage is best for items you use weekly or less often.

CLASSIC CABINETRY

Out of sight shouldn't be out of mind in the bathroom. Tame the space inside drawers with partitions, trays, bins, and bags. Pullout shelves installed on the bottom of cabinets give you a bird's-eye view of everything stashed under the sink. Wire, plastic, and wood are economical and easy to install yourself—or you can have a carpenter construct custom-size pullouts with heavy-duty sliding hardware. Either way, look for tiered options that work with your plumbing.

PARTNER VANITY

Two sinks in a bath are a wonderful convenience, but the extra space means extra planning. Assign ownership or specific responsibilities to each bar, drawer, and compartment around a sink. "No one can maintain an organizing routine unless it includes designated spaces," professional organizer Laura Leist says. Shared items (perhaps toothpaste or a stack of washcloths) belong in shared areas, while personal items need separate drawers or containers.

challenges | linens

Lean linen storage is the first step to a well-organized bath. Conduct a thorough review of your towels and sheets today.

Keep just enough towels and washcloths in your linen closet for one to two weeks of regular use, and strive for consistency. "A mix of towels just feels cluttered, making it harder for you to feel organized," professional organizer Laura Leist says. Pare down to or purchase just one or two colors of linens with similar thicknesses. Fold everything the same way. Position linens at eye level or slightly above, sharing shelves with frequently used toiletries.

Only stock towels that are in great condition.
Use old towels for pets, as rags, or to wash your car.

1. PERFECT PILES

Use shelf dividers designed for sweaters to keep stacks of linens standing tall. For a clean look, fold consistently and face the rounded edge out so items are easy to grab.

2. PRACTICAL PIECES

If your bath lacks a closet, repurpose a cabinet—or, in this case, a vintage vanity and hutch topper with glass-front doors—to organize towels and extra supplies.

3. BAND TOGETHER

A ribbon belt secures a complete set of sheets. Storing soaps nearby imparts a fresh scent to laundered linens.

4. TRADING SPACES

Outfit a cabinet compartment with X-shape dividers and fill with rolled towels.

5. STACKS & RACKS

Wire stands subdivide a collection of mixed sheet sets and bath linens by type. The stands' open design encourages airflow. Towel bars mounted inside the closet door present the prettiest linens for guests.

challenges | personal items

Easy adaptations to fit your routine let you pamper yourself in little ways, day or night.

Grooming is much more pleasant when you know exactly where every product, tool, and finishing touch belongs. Frequency of use is the key to determining where to stow toiletries. Items you use every day need to be kept in the open or be accessible in one movement (opening the medicine cabinet, for example). Items used weekly should involve no more than two movements (opening a low drawer and lifting a caddy). Infrequently used items can be stored in more remote areas—just not so out-of-sight that you forget about them.

save money

Try professional organizer Laura Leist's "shop from home" strategy to manage excess toiletries: Gather excess products in bins you store in a nearby closet. Visit this stash before you go to a store.

1. SORTED LIFE
Place cosmetics in a divided acrylic organizer. A clear container allows you to see contents from all angles.

2. HOLE IN ONE
A deep vanity drawer is custom-fit with a wood insert with metal silverware bins (available at restaurant supply stores), safely allowing unplugged hair-care tools to cool.

3. SECRET STORAGE
A pantry pullout cabinet designed for spices serves just as well for grooming products. Three levels of shelving are accessible from both sides and from above.

4. MORE FROM DOORS
Put cabinet openings to work by hanging canvas pouches on the inside and adding an over-the-door holder as an extra towel bar.

5. ON THE RACK
Slatted closet storage components work well as bath furniture, offering ventilated storage for toiletries and towels. Ceramic flowerpots hold razors and brushes.

challenges | wet storage

Getting clean is easy when your sink, tub, or shower is properly equipped. Splish-splash away!

Your bath's wet areas are its work zones, so outfit them appropriately. Store only essential tools and supplies there and forgo the fussy stuff.

But you don't have to sacrifice style. More water-friendly storage solutions and containers are appearing every year. Start with plastic options, as they're appropriate for users of any age and are usually dishwasher-safe. Expand your shopping to include bamboo and teak, as well as stainless steel and rubber-coated wire.

Keep only shampoos and soaps you use regularly inside the shower. Stow all other bottles elsewhere.

1. DRIPPY DELIGHT
An expandable plastic basket corrals bath toys and kid shampoos. Slats allow items to dry when bath time is done.

2. RESTING ROUNDS
Get bottles off the floor and tub edge by building in ceramic shelves in a corner. For a budget-savvy approach, affix wire or plastic shelving with suction cups.

3. BENCH BUDDY
A teak stool next to the tub is a prime spot for scrubbing tools, bath salts, or beverages. A single open shelf holds towels for when it's time to dry off.

4. DRYING STATION
Attach a bar to the side of a cabinet, clearing the countertop and creating a place for wet towels and washcloths.

5. SHELF LIFE
Wrap two waterproof ledges in the corner of a shower to accommodate tall or bulk-size shampoo and conditioner bottles.

before & after

A systemic upgrade of a basic vanity makes this couple's mornings brisk and happy.

BEFORE
problems

Though they started with a double vanity, Lindsey and Aaron's messy undersink area caused them to repeatedly bump into each other as they reached for toiletries. The couple tried to employ bins and baskets, but without labels or a clear hierarchy, they found themselves digging through the cabinets every day in search of essential items.

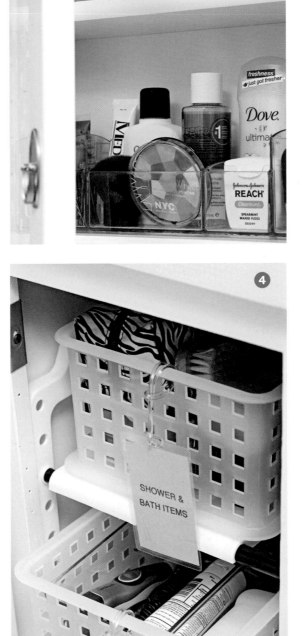

solutions

To speed up Lindsey and Aaron's morning routine, professional organizer Lorie Marrero had the couple remove everything from the room, sort toiletries by frequency of use, hang a cabinet for each homeowner, and place daily necessities at the front of the cabinets. "It's no longer stressful to be in our bathroom together," Lindsey says.

1 Slender wall-mount cabinets maximize the vanity's limited sidewalls. An integrated towel bar gives each homeowner a spot to dry hands.

2 Skinny acrylic containers steady a bevy of medicine, floss, and first aid products inside the shallow wall cabinets.

3 Metal pails hold daily needs such as cotton balls and swabs on a bamboo tray that is a cinch to wipe clean.

4 To prevent bumping into each other, Lindsey and Aaron designated one sink and undercabinet area per person. Inside, they filled plastic baskets with personal items. Plastic luggage tags ensure the new system stays in check.

get going now

Quick fixes make a world of difference. Incorporate these time-saving ideas into your bath routine.

1 Sort linens by room, type, or person and then arrange in stacks on shelves. Keep everything in place with metal wire shelf dividers and finish off with labels applied to the shelf edge.

2 Mount a shallow shelf in the sliver of space between sink and mirror and use it as a spot for toothbrushes and other daily items.

3 Rest toiletries on a small tray that you can lift instantly for quick cleaning or tuck away when guests arrive.

4 Fashion a manicure kit by filling a caddy with nail supplies. Use a similar approach with cosmetics, hair-care tools, or spa essentials.

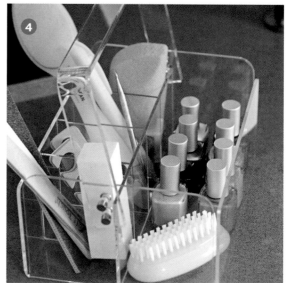

If you don't have a day to organize your entire bathroom, dedicate 15 minutes to tackling one vanity drawer.

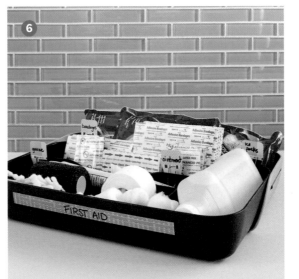

5 Group cleaning supplies on a pullout shelf in the base of your vanity. Fit scrub brushes and smaller items in baskets.

6 Arrange bandages and ointments in a utensil tray to serve as a first aid kit. Clip on file tabs to identify items.

7 Assign an individual tote to each family member to take to the shower or place on the counter while primping. Choose lightweight, scrubbable acrylic or plastic and affix adhesive name labels.

8 Install an L-shape pullout rack to accommodate the plumbing under your sink. Arrange toiletries file-style so you can see options without bending over. Load mini-buckets with cosmetics.

bedrooms & closets

Turn your dream of a serene sleep space and a streamlined closet into reality with smart solutions to organize clothing, accessories, and more.

A bedroom that balances function and relaxation can be yours when you answer these questions. **How do you use the space?** Having some work supplies or a television in a bedroom is fine, but know what you want from the room and then establish clear divisions between zones for dressing, working, relaxing, and sleeping. **How do you store clothing?** Let your preference for folding, hanging, or some combination of the two lead your efforts to shape your closets and dressers. **What do you actually use?** Rigorously edit your clothing, as well as your bedside reading pile and displayed mementos. Give space only to items you need and truly love.

ultimate master suite

This smartly planned cluster of spaces for sleeping, dressing, relaxing, and grooming ensures more than a good night's sleep.

A REPURPOSED sideboard is a pretty storage solution in this master suite's sitting area, with baskets to hold magazines and drawers for hidden storage.

A bevy of built-ins, smart clothing storage, and a shipshape bath combine to create a full-service retreat.

Lacquered boxes *top left* store fragile items such as eyeglasses and special jewelry. Fresh socks and T-shirts are at the ready thanks to canvas dividers.

A built-in dresser *top right* adds charm to a dormer window. Pants and sweaters stay neatly stowed inside, while the top surface acts as a display niche for photos.

A multidrawer dresser *far left* offers more storage than a traditional nightstand. A pullout tray provides a place for reading material.

Built-in bath shelving *left* boasts clear apothecary jars filled with cotton balls and bath salts. The shelves adjust to accommodate larger items.

A double vanity *below left* features slow-close doors and furniture-style details. A small metal tray gathers daily essentials while cabinets hide grooming supplies and personal items.

ultimate master suite

A modular closet system *opposite* **combines hanging bars, open cubby storage, and drawers to organize clothing. A curved dressing bench takes up less space than a rectangular one.**

Over-door hooks *above right* **are a spot to assemble an outfit or air-dry items.**

Matching canvas boxes *above, far right* **with discreet labels hold extra sheet sets. Comforters and pillows air out on open shelves above.**

An ironing station *right* **unfurls for quick touch-ups. Nearby wicker baskets store ironing supplies.**

A simple metal rack *far right* **is a space-saving solution that makes it easy to find the perfect necktie.**

in the zone

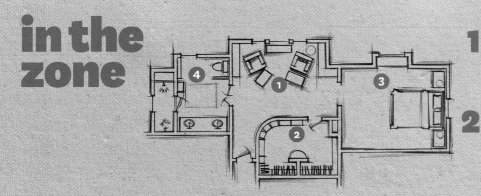

1 A sitting room with two chairs and a storage-friendly sideboard calms the master suite entry.

2 The master closet employs shelving, rods, and drawers to organize clothing for two.

3 A built-in dresser and nightstands with drawers simplify the sleeping space.

4 Built-in shelving near the shower combines bins and baskets for orderly grooming supplies.

ultimate walk-in closet

Stacking up stock components creates a custom look in this 8×10-foot master closet.

OPEN SHELVES
hold bulky items and pretty storage boxes while cabinet doors and drawers hide mess. A wall shelf mounts inside the door for grab-and-go accessory storage.

Think of ready-to-assemble storage pieces as building blocks you can arrange and rearrange to suit your needs.

Foam organizers
above, far right **sort earrings, bracelets, and rings. Extra drawer space is perfect for wallets and small clutches.**

Thin metal bars
right **keep shoes secure yet accessible on slanted shelves. The rack holds up to a dozen pairs of women's shoes.**

A wire hamper
far right **is cleverly hidden behind a tilt-out cabinet front. A mesh bag on the shelf above collects delicate items and can be thrown into the washing machine.**

A special wood hanger
below right **prevents scarves from getting tangled or snagged in a drawer.**

Zip-top fabric bins
below, far right **protect extra blankets and sheets from dust and add fun flair to closet shelves.**

charging station

socks

his

A pullout rack *opposite* with dowels prevents wrinkles on up to a dozen pairs of trousers. A mix of fabric bins and plastic boxes holds sweaters, accessories, and bedding.

Phones and electronics *right* recharge overnight in a drawer charging station. A power strip installed in the back of the drawer means cords can stay put. Watches and other everyday necessities stow nearby.

A pullout valet bar *below right* supports clothes while ironing or preparing tomorrow's outfit. Monogrammed wood hangers add a personal touch.

A fold-out ironing board *below, far right* makes pressing garments a breeze. An outlet on the back wall means irons and steamers can be stored below.

in the zone

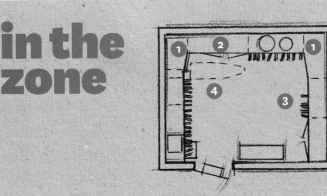

1 Corner shelving units outfitted with bins and boxes provide floor-to-ceiling storage.

2 Pullout shelves with modular organizers sort folded clothing and accessories. Rub-on letters are easy to affix and revise.

3 A mirror nestled inside a tall cubby functions as a place to try on jewelry and other finishing touches.

4 A compact hamper means fewer trips to the laundry room. Nearby supplies allow for pretreating stains and ironing.

small-space bedroom

A small sleeping space gets a fashionable, functional makeover with clever custom touches.

A WELL-APPOINTED bed is the centerpiece of this storage-rich room. Lidded baskets underneath store extra sheets and seasonal clothing.

A reach-in closet
above left **gets a storage boost thanks to stock closet components purchased from a home improvement store. Cubbies house baskets of accessories, while less-pretty items hide in drawers and behind cabinet doors.**

A storage headboard
above center **offers up an unexpected place to stow extra blankets, books, or even office supplies for the nearby vanity/desk. The top surface is wide enough for a telephone or a few decorative items.**

An upcycled dresser
above right **finds new life as a nightstand and holds magazines and personal items. The bottom drawer was removed, and its compartment was converted to a simple shelf for books and a tissue box.**

save space

Writing desks and sofa tables hug the wall, doubling as office and vanity areas. Complement one of these pieces with a backless seat and wall-mount shelves to maximize function in a tight space.

small smarts

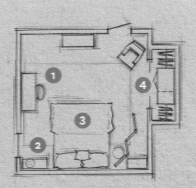

1 A slim desk and a storage ottoman double as a vanity and mini-office.

2 A flea market dresser becomes a hardworking nightstand when a coat of paint is applied and the bottom drawer is removed.

3 A headboard compartment hides extra amenities. Space underneath the bed is packed with baskets of sheets and clothing.

4 Stacked ready-to-assemble storage components look like built-in cabinets within the closet.

small-space reach-in closet

Wire shelving and budget-friendly organizers turned this one-rod closet into a hub for inspiring organization.

DRY CLEANING

HIS

HIS

DRESSER DRAWER units and shoe cubbies hang from vertical runners. The space above a pair of drawers functions as a vanity surface for primping.

Inject style quickly into any closet with color-coordinated bins.

Adhesive labels *above right* **are a temporary way to distinguish between contents of fabric bins.**

Lidded containers *above, far right* **protect accessories that aren't worn on a daily basis. Front handles make the boxes easy to pull down from a high shelf.**

Clear acrylic boxes *right* **with drop-down fronts are ideal for showing off shoes.**

A jewelry stand *far right* **adds personal verve to the closet. The tiered design holds bracelets and necklaces, while small holes accommodate earrings.**

Canvas drawer dividers *below right* **maximize storage for socks and undergarments. A small sachet imparts a sweet scent.**

A collapsible stool *below, far right* **optimizes high shelf storage. This stool folds flat and slips underneath the shoe shelf when not in use.**

small-space reach-in closet

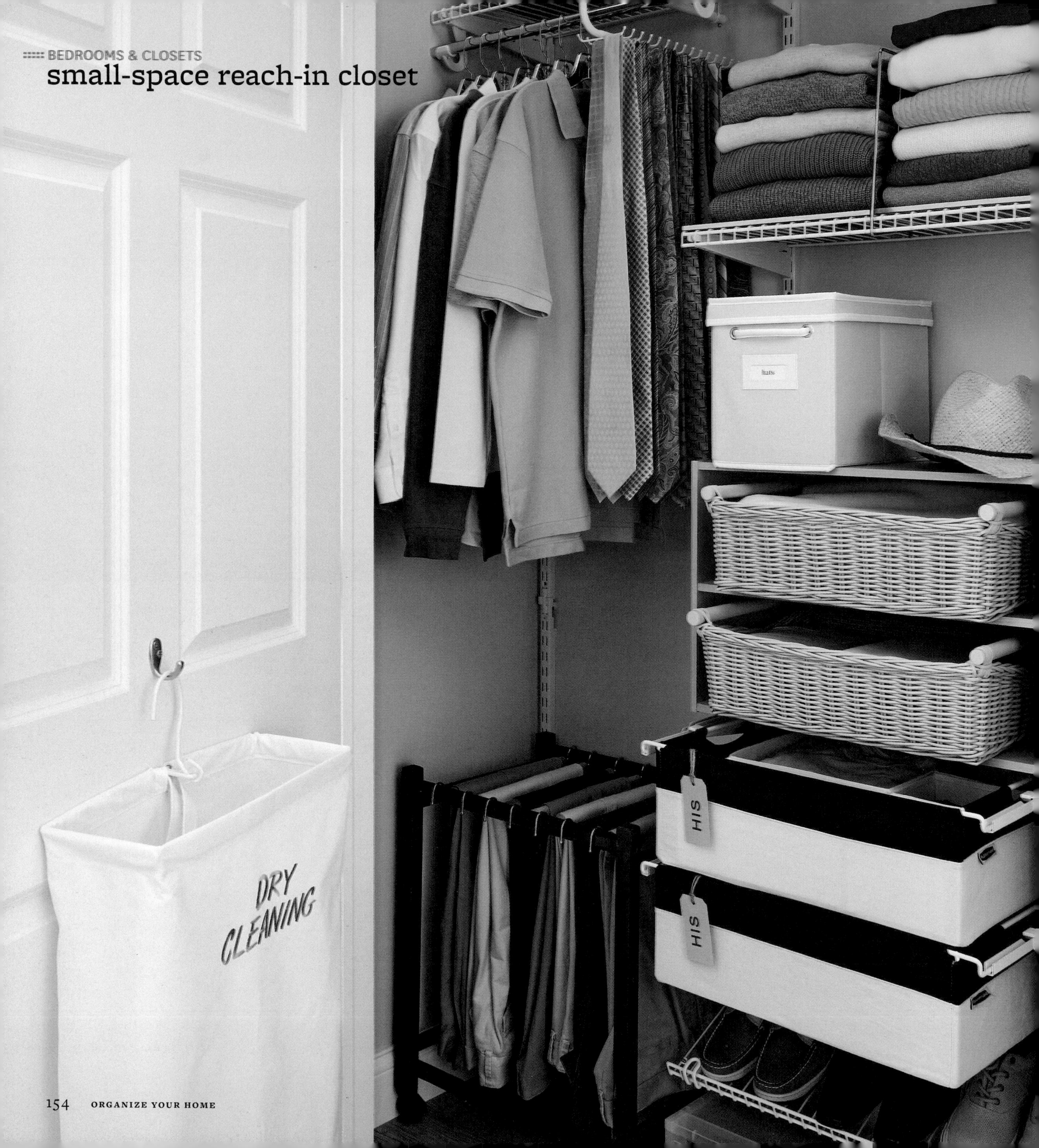

DRY CLEANING

HIS

HIS

A rolling trolley *opposite* neatly stores slacks on cedar posts and adds an upscale touch to the closet.

A metal rack *above right* snaps to the underside of a wire shelf, providing quick access to ties or other accessories. The rack can easily move elsewhere in the closet as necessary.

A chrome divider *right* clips onto a wire shelf to steady stacks of folded sweaters. Premade pallets of cedar defend knitwear from moths and other pests.

Pullout canvas drawers *far right* subdivided by canvas bins sort socks, T-shirts, and undergarments. Hanging tags add a personal touch.

small smarts

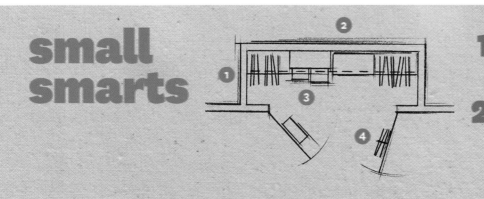

1 Short hanging bars on either side of the closet accommodate shirts and skirts.

2 A shelf tucked into the top of the closet hosts bins and boxes filled with extra linens and less-used accessories.

3 Delicates and undergarments are stored discreetly in wood and canvas drawers.

4 The insides of the closet doors pitch in with a hanging hamper and a rod for full-length clothing.

essential elements | bedrooms

Bedrooms may be for restful slumber, but supporting pieces in a sleep space must be as dynamic as any furniture in your home.

BEDSIDE STORAGE

Matching nightstands and lamps flanking the bed provide a classic look, but feel free to make substitutions in the interest of improved organization. Swap out a pretty but impractical table for a small cabinet, writing desk, or bookshelf. Fill large open spaces with baskets or bins that stabilize stacks of linens or reading material. Optimize the top by replacing lamps with sconces and adding a tray for necessities that's easy to lift when dusting.

DRESSERS

Chests and bureaus are bedroom storage staples, but they frequently frustrate homeowners. "The contents within a dresser just aren't as visible as on open shelving," professional organizer Lorie Marrero says. "You end up rooting through and making a jumble." Introduce order by storing only one type of item in each drawer, then add stabilizing dividers. Shop for expandable plastic or wood versions, or go the DIY route and cut apart shoeboxes to fashion barriers.

Out-of-sight storage is restful, but don't lose track of where you stashed stuff.

UNDER-THE-BED SOLUTIONS

A typical twin-size bed offers more than 20 cubic feet of storage between the box spring and floor. Unlock the potential of this space by selecting a bed frame that includes built-in drawers or sliding several lidded boxes under the bed. The underbed area is best for storing off-season items, such as sweaters, boots, and linens, or infrequently used items such as craft supplies, gift wrap, and mementos you can't quite let go of.

ACCESSORY STORAGE

Little bits take up room physically—and psychologically. Before you purchase special holders, boxes, and racks for finishing touches, do a rigorous evaluation and ask yourself why you're holding onto things. "Accessories can have a lot of emotion attached to them," Marrero says. "Don't keep things around that make you feel bad. Of course, you can keep historically significant items, but you need to use or display them in places of honor in your home."

essential elements | closets

Take closets to the next level by supplementing hanging bars with helpful extras. The results may look so good, you'll want to forgo doors.

DRAWERS

Tired of wasting precious time crisscrossing your bedroom while getting dressed each morning? The simplest solution may be to introduce a few drawers into your closet for staples such as underwear and socks. Closet systems at most price points feature add-on drawer units made of various materials, including wood, canvas, wire, and wicker. Or simply slide a small dresser or cabinet under a section of short hanging clothes to give yourself a few drawers.

OPEN SHELVES

When you can see it, you're much more likely to wear it. "A stack of folded clothes on a shelf is more visible than the same stack in a drawer," professional organizer Lorie Marrero says. To prevent everything from toppling over, Marrero relies on shelf dividers between piles and teaches the "pancake flipper" method of managing stacks: Insert your hand flat like a spatula above the item of clothing you want, lift the stack, get the item you want, and gently put the stack back down.

"You need to be in the right frame of mind to edit your closet. You may be able to get there yourself, but it's almost always better with the help of an honest friend."

—**Lorie Marrero,** professional organizer

SPECIALTY ORGANIZING ADD-ONS

Closet systems at every price point now include add-on elements for shoes, pants, accessories, and more. Marrero encourages clients to thoroughly examine an add-on before purchasing. Imagine yourself using the element. Test it in the store, if possible. Does it seem durable? Most important, how visible and accessible will the add-on make your clothes? "Even if it saves space, you need to be able to see your clothes if you're ever going wear them," Marrero says.

HANGERS

All joking about wire hangers aside, don't skimp on these storage essentials. A sturdy wood, plastic, or metal hanger that minimizes wrinkles and maintains a garment's natural shape will last for decades. Invest in enough good-quality hangers to take care of your current clothing storage needs, plus 20 percent more to allow for new acquisitions. Struggling with a shared closet? Improve function by designating a specific hanger color or finish for each user.

challenges | clothes

Piles of clothing are the quickest way to disrupt a serene bedroom. Try these tips to establish and maintain order.

Everything you keep in your closet should fit three criteria: It's a current or classic style, it fits you perfectly, and you've worn it in the past year.

After you finish editing and restocking your closet, turn every hanger backward. As you wear and rehang items, turn their hangers the correct way. Over the course of a season, you'll find out what you actually wear—and next season's editing will be that much easier.

If visible labels don't appeal to you, try marking the inside of drawers and cabinets to encourage tidy storage.

1. JEAN SCENE
Take a cue from department stores and stock denim by cut or style. You'll never again need to pull out every pair to find the one you're looking for.

2. CLEVER CUBES
Cubbies are great for storing sweaters, sweatshirts, and T-shirts. Place the items you wear most often on low shelves and save dresser drawers for more personal items. Fold consistently so each garment is easy to identify and grab.

3. BONUS ROD
Save yourself from last-minute rifling by installing a valet rod that extends from the side of a wardrobe. It's the ideal spot for garments fresh from dry-cleaning or those you plan to iron or pack.

4. ALL SYSTEMS GO
Customize your closet system to fit your lifestyle. Here, suit jackets and dress shirts take up most of the available space, while tees and athletic wear warrant only a few open shelves.

5. SEASON SAVVY
Keep seasonal items in similar, clearly labeled baskets. Position swim gear or sandals prominently during warm months, then swap the entire basket for one filled with tights or gloves when the weather gets chilly.

save time
It's OK to break a closet-organizing project into chunks, spending 15 minutes focusing on only shirts or shoes. Many people, however, get into a groove when evaluating clothing, so plan to dedicate an afternoon to editing an entire closet.

challenges | accessories

Well-structured storage keeps purses, jewelry, and ties from getting lost in a sea of clutter.

All those finishing touches are just that—personal flourishes you add at the very end of getting dressed. With this in mind, move your accessories out of your main clothing storage area and establish a primping station. Yours may be the top of a dresser, a corner of your bath vanity, a portion of a desk, or a spot near the door. Display your accessories on racks, stands, or hooks so you can see all your options. Outfit with a mirror, good lighting, and your favorite cosmetics.

bags

scarves

ask a pro
Objectivity is crucial when editing your clothing. "A pro can ask gently how long has it been since you last wore something," professional organizer Lorie Marrero says. "She's like a best friend— but an honest best friend."

1. GLASS APPEAL
Storing accessories behind glass-panel doors encourages you to tidy up frequently. Coat hooks mounted to the sides of these repurposed kitchen cabinets helpfully hold ties and scarves.

2. TRINKETS TROVE
Tiny baubles are easy to lose. Use a muffin tin or petite bowls to house pairs of earrings and tangle-prone necklaces.

3. MAKE-UP WORK
Instead of tossing all your makeup into a bag, separate cosmetics by type in wood, acrylic, or metal desk drawer organizers. Stand brushes in a shapely glass or vase filled with sand or pebbles.

4. CRIMP-FREE
Roll ties and belts to avoid wrinkles and other distortions. Place in a divided caddy, sorted by color or occasion.

5. CHICKEN OUT
Attach chicken wire to the inside of a dresser door for an inexpensive jewelry holder.

challenges | shoes

If you're a shoe lover, pay attention to how you shelve your prized pairs with these strategies for heels, flats, and more.

It's a puzzle worthy of Solomon: How many shoes is too many? "The exact number is so subjective," professional organizer Lorie Marrero says. "If you have the space, you can have more pairs. The real problem, whatever your capacity, is overflow." Marrero recommends establishing an area for frequently used footwear and strictly adhering to a one-in/one-out policy for this zone. Stow off-season and specialty footwear on a high shelf or in a secondary closet to squeeze in a few extra pairs.

Store your everyday shoes as close to eye level as possible, and stock consistently, with either heels or toes facing out.

1. SEASONAL STOW
Extra cabinet space? Organize by season and stow away shoes that won't be worn for another six months.

2. SOLE SORTER
Store off-season shoes one layer deep in a labeled underbed bin outfitted with expandable drawer dividers. For easiest access, choose a clear container with wheels and a split lid.

3. ON DISPLAY
Treat your prettiest pairs as works of art. This convenient shoe rail is constructed of two pieces of wood molding and offers about 2 inches of depth to safely secure most heels to the wall.

4. FANTASTIC PLASTIC
Replace original cardboard boxes with clear ones so you can see exactly what's in every container. Fold-down front openings mean you don't have to unstack to get to your favorites.

5. MIX MASTER
Outfit a shoe closet with both cubby- and shelf-style components. Flats and sandals can double up in cubbies, while chunky heels (and wider men's shoes) are easier to store on undivided shelves.

before & after

A couple maximizes a tiny
clothes closet by implementing
savvy space-planning strategies.

BEFORE
problems

Bruce and Meredith
bought their home
because they fell in
love with its historical
character, but small
storage spaces left them
with a jumble of clothes
in their master closet.
The 20×69-inch space
was crowded, while
a fixed shelf wasted
potential storage space
above. Without a clear
system, the couple found
themselves putting away
clean laundry wherever
it fit, only perpetuating
their storage woes.

solutions

Professional organizer Lorie Marrero had Bruce and Meredith use her A-B-C-D organizing method to clean up their space and prioritize placement for every item. "A" items—those used daily—remained in the closet, along with "B" items, used weekly. However, "C" and "D" items, used only occasionally or seasonally, respectively, found new homes elsewhere in the house.

1 The couple traded curtains for closet doors, gaining extra storage space for Meredith's shoes on one door.

2 Wire mesh baskets were installed to hold Bruce's socks and underwear, which formerly lived in a dresser across the room.

3 Slim matching hangers save space and feature a velvety finish to keep clothes from slipping.

4 Flip-out hooks, mounted on the inside of a closet door, store belts.

get going now

A few quick upgrades can increase the function of your closet, dressers, and bedside tables tenfold.

1 Slip plastic placemats or laminated squares of scrapbooking paper between folded sweaters. Each garment slides out easily without disrupting the stack.

2 Keep extra linens out of sight but easy to reach in a labeled underbed basket. Include a dryer sheet or cedar block to preserve freshness.

3 Organize sheet sets by room, using bookends and clipped-on labels to keep everything in place.

4 Cut PVC pipe into 3- or 4-inch-tall segments and position in a drawer. Roll up ties, scarves, or belts and deposit in individual compartments.

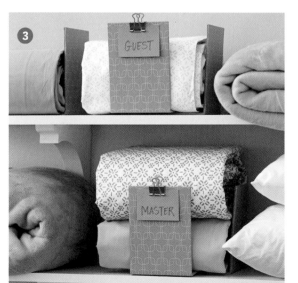

When using trays and other open storage, only display items you use daily to keep surfaces as tidy as possible.

5 Replace a few drawers in a flea market dresser with punchy-color baskets. Fill with accessories, socks, or undergarments. Tie a numbered tag to the outside to keep track of what's inside.

6 Display perfume, makeup, and jewelry on a divided ceramic tray. Introduce levels by adding a few appetizer bowls, tumblers, or pastry stands.

7 Collect shoe polishes and sprays in a partitioned valet box and store near your shoe collection. Include a brush, extra laces, and heel pads for fast fixes.

8 Organize your hanging clothing by type and add hanger tags to ensure you keep like with like.

kids' spaces

They may be small, but kids sure come with a lot of stuff. Set up systems that put young ones in charge of managing their own toys, clothes, and gear.

Get your child—and your home—more organized by considering the following questions. **What example are you setting?** Before complaining about a child, take a look at yourself. As a parent, you need to model the style and level of organization you're seeking. **What do you expect?** Just like adults, kids need to know exactly what they need to do in order to be successful. Rather than edicts and threats, you'll get better results with clear guidelines such as, "In our home, we only wash clothes that have been placed in a hamper." **How flexible can you be?** Your child may never maintain a picture-perfect room. Can you settle for having everything off the floor by bedtime every night?

ultimate kid bedroom

Playful and practical come together in a room that inspires a child's creativity and satisfies a parent's need for neatness.

CUSTOM BOOKCASES give this small bedroom a window seat. Doors that resemble windowpanes hide shelves filled with toys and books.

A mirrored cabinet *above right* provides a special place for dress-up clothes and accessories. The adjacent side features hooks for purses and cubbies for shoes.

A pullout board *above, far right* features dowels for storing puppets upright. The unit hides behind an acrylic windowpane.

Chalkboard paint *right* adds a fun, versatile touch to kids' rooms. Here, bins with chalkboard fronts make sorting toys a snap.

Stock storage units *far right* replace a low bar for storing clothes in the closet. As a child ages, the configuration can change to accommodate longer-hanging clothes.

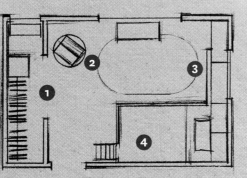

in the zone

1 Ready-to-assemble drawers are stacked in the closet to store small clothing.

2 A rotating cabinet separates dress-up clothes from everyday wear. Hooks, cubbies, and bins sort accessories.

3 A storage unit built around the window features cubbies for toys and a burgeoning library.

4 A loft bed maximizes floor space, creating room for a playhouse underneath.

ultimate teen sleep space

A single-function teen bedroom is transformed into a flexible space suited for relaxing, studying, and creating.

A TWIN-SIZE DAYBED outfitted with underbed drawers and two low bookshelves saves space. A chalkboard wall frames the bed and provides a place to jot reminders.

Super-easy storage *above, far left* **is key to maintaining a tidy teen room. Three matching wall shelves with hooks hang side-by-side above the bed. The ledge displays collections and art; the hooks deal with clothing and bags.**

A mix of storage boxes *below, far left* **hold folded clothing, accessories, and electronics. A file box resting on top of the unit,** *opposite,* **is turned on its back and serves as a drop spot for papers.**

Shallow plastic bins *left* **nest within each other, organizing crafts supplies in one of the underbed drawers. Labels on the drawer interior designate contents.**

Teens are more likely to stay organized when you give them a say in storage strategies.

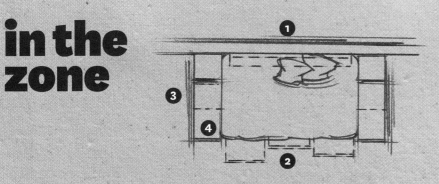

in the zone

1 Chalkboard paint, shelving, and sconces combine as a fun, functional backdrop.

2 Underbed drawers and flanking bookshelves for clothing and craft supplies supplement the daybed.

3 Translucent bins help a teen manage school supplies, electronics, and jewelry.

4 Working on projects is easy with a small bedside toolbox filled with frequently used art and office supplies.

ultimate playroom

Versatile furniture and effortless storage make this cozy basement playroom a prime place for kids and teens to gather.

SLIDING PANELS
mask a 15-inch-deep media hub that uses shelves, cubbies, and glass-front console cabinets to manage DVDs, music, and gaming gear.

Rectangular benches
left are assigned to each family member, providing personal storage spots. These wheeled units combine open cubbies and drawers for maximum flexibility. Drilled holes eliminate the need for potentially dangerous drawer knobs.

Cube units
below left forgo the pillows and seat cushions to function as rolling end tables. The drawers slide out on either side to increase access to books and games.

save money

Choosing versatile containers lets you easily switch contents and functions as children age. The same plastic bin in this room can hold soft toys for a toddler, a play set for a young child, and games for an older child.

in the zone

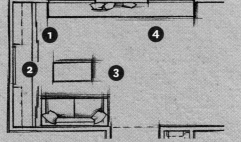

1 Fabric panels hide a flat-panel TV, stereo equipment, and gaming consoles.

2 A mix of off-the-rack benches, boxes, and shelves wrap around the television and span the wall, giving this area the look of custom cabinetry.

3 A chest-style coffee table hides blankets and board games. The top is tough enough for frequent use.

4 Four wheeled units can move throughout the room or line a wall as an upholstered bench for lounging.

essential elements

It's never to late to introduce organizing tools. Regardless of age, your child will benefit from using these all-purpose storage solutions.

STORAGE THAT GROWS

Whenever you purchase furniture or containers for your child, do a little mental time traveling. How might your kid use this item in a year? In five years? In 10 years? Good storage solutions have timeless style, are made of durable materials, and easily adjust to hold various types of toys, clothing, or sporting gear. If a drawer and cubby seems too vast for your toddler, add on some temporary dividers or mini shelves to break the area into smaller spaces for tinier items.

LABELS

Kids change as they age, and so do their label needs. Look for options that are easy to update and revise, such as vinyl pockets, blank stickers, and rewritable tags. Start toddlers early with picture labels. As your child matures, opt for labels that combine words and images. By age 10 or so, most children prefer text-only labels. At this point, begin empowering them to make their own labels by teaching them how to fill in blank templates or use an electronic label maker.

save money

Money management teaches kids organization and responsibility. Start early with a bank. As kids age, move to three jars labeled "spend," "save," and "give." Open a checking account for tweens and teens.

OPEN STORAGE

Toy boxes might be classic kid furniture, but some adjustable shelves and kid-friendly containers do a better job of managing playtime gear. "If you want little kids to put things away, access has to be easy-easy," professional organizer Kathy Jenkins says. Stash soft-sided, lidless bins on the lowest shelves of a bookcase or built-in. Make sure there's about 6 inches of access above the containers' lips, so everyone can quickly drop in errant toys at cleanup time.

CLEAR CONTAINERS

Being able to see what's inside a plastic or acrylic container yields myriad benefits. Most notably, the contents themselves serve as instant "labels." Even though small pieces still collect in the bottom, you can always see them and know whether you need to empty the box or bin to find what you're looking for. And clear containers are a help to grandparents, sitters, and other caregivers who might have no idea where to find your daughter's favorite pink doll shoes.

challenges | clothes

Keep clothing off the floor with these kid-friendly ideas for dressers and closets.

Minimizing kid clothing chaos is all about getting youngsters to buy in. "Talk with your children about how they want to set up things," professional organizer Kathy Jenkins says. Even with very young kids, you can ask them where they like to get dressed and whether they prefer their school clothes to hang on the right or left side of their closets. "The exact place for these things doesn't really matter, but kids have some ownership in setting up the system. And if they help make the system, they can be accountable for keeping up their closets," Jenkins says.

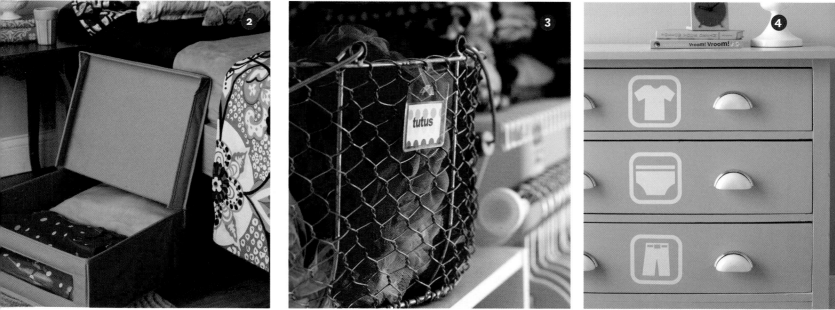

Consider removing a kid's closet doors and replacing them with a tension rod, rings, and a curtain panel.

1. READY TO GO

Before bed each night, help your child set out all the elements for the next day's outfit. Use a canvas bag to gather shoes, socks, and accessories.

2. SLIP SLIDE AWAY

Reserve underbed boxes in a kid's room for off-season clothing. Choose containers with split lids so retrieving garments is quick and easy.

3. RELAXED ORDER

Don't force kids to fold unnecessarily. Some garments—socks, undergarments, cold-weather gear, play clothes—are best stored in bins or baskets that kids can dig through.

4. FIND IT FASTER

Minimize rooting for that favorite T-shirt by adding labels to drawer exteriors. Use a similar strategy to indicate whose clothing goes where in a shared chest.

5. UP & DOWN

Outfit a kid's closet with vertical runners and an array of bars, shelves, and drawers that you can adjust to match your child's size and the items you're storing. Designate the lowest bar or shelf for everyday items your child is responsible for; use higher spots for dress clothes and seasonal items.

challenges | playtime & homework

Organization is important at all ages. Long-term storage solutions are key as children grow from tots to teens.

As children age, the size of their toys shrinks—but the sheer number of toys may seem to expand exponentially. Parents need to take the lead in combating excess kid stuff. Encourage your child to pick and display favorites, then regift or donate lesser stuffed animals, dolls, or trucks.

Even better, stop the buildup before it begins by forgoing toy gifts in favor of activity gifts such as pool passes, museum memberships, ball game tickets, and gift certificates for lessons or activities your child enjoys.

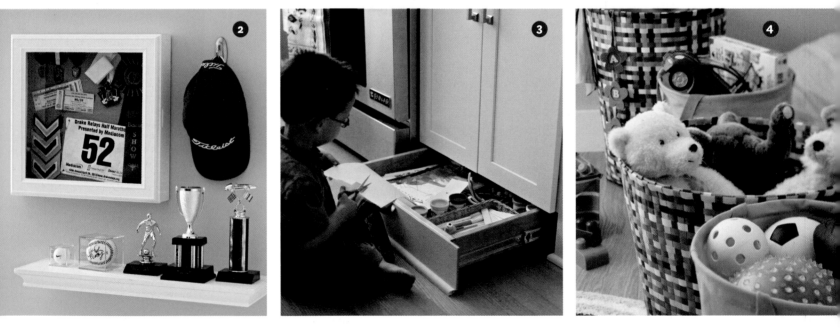

Establish a 10-minute tidy-up routine before bedtime. Set a timer and make sure every family member participates.

ask a pro

Around age 10, kids are ready to start weeding out toys. "Letting kids grow up can be difficult," professional organizer Kathy Jenkins says. "But it's a time to encourage them to make decisions about what stays in their rooms."

1. NOW & LATER

Adjustable shelving and desks can be rearranged as children grow and needs change. These workspaces are currently positioned for 4-year-olds to engage in art activities and games. Later they can be raised to support laptop computers and homework.

2. ALL ABOUT ME

Showcase memories and top achievements in an easy-to-open shadow box. Display trophies and collectibles on shallow ledges. Affix adhesive hangers to display hats and other hangable items.

3. BUDDING ARTIST

Outfit unused toe-kick space in a kitchen or utility-room cabinet with a drawer for construction paper and art supplies.

4. TAKEAWAY

Work with toddlers' natural interest in emptying and filling by encouraging them to help you place toys in soft-sided bins and baskets. Just be sure to put away the filled container before your toddler empties it again.

5. CHALKED UP

Encourage responsibility by hanging a mix of organizing tools in a child's room, including magnetic dry-erase boards, cork panels, wall pockets, and some type of calendar.

before & after

Efficient storage systems and kid-friendly labeling help this family carve out an inviting playroom.

BEFORE
problems

Heather and Leroy's children, Jack, 6, and Katie, 2, loved playing in the basement family room. But without a defined strategy for storing toys, the space often became a chaotic mess that threatened to engulf the nearby media area. Heather and Leroy tried employing large plastic tubs, but the kids' smaller toys got lost in the bottoms, making it hard for them to find their favorites.

> "Now everyone knows where everything goes, so the entire family takes a more active role in the cleanup process."
>
> —**Heather,** homeowner

solutions

The first thing professional organizer Donna Smallin had Heather and Leroy do was thoroughly appraise their children's toys. Items that hadn't been played with in the past six months were donated or sold, while other toys were sorted by type—puppets, superheroes, and race cars, for instance. The couple then designated a dedicated "play and pack up" zone, separating the play area from the rest of the family room.

1 Wall-mount cubby units leave floor space for storing larger toys below.

2 Large stuffed animals and odd-shape plastic toys find homes in soft-sided baskets. Hanging labels identify contents.

3 The couple outfitted each bin and basket with a label that included both text and pictures so their young children could help clean up.

4 A freestanding bookcase, placed behind a sofa in the adjacent living space, reinforces a border for the play zone. Bins hide small and medium-size toys.

get going now

Simple strategies can help children of any age better manage their toys, supplies, and clothing.

1 Use a tray to establish a drop zone for accessories, wallets, cologne, and deodorant in a teen's room. The tray protects the dresser top, and with everything out in the open, morning routines are a breeze.

2 Sort art supplies by project and place in handled plastic bins that travel easily and stack to save space.

3 Evaluate children's clothing on a seasonal basis, giving away items that no longer fit. Inventory items you're keeping by attaching adhesive labels to plastic bins. Include notes on items you'll need to purchase next year.

4 Frame your kid's art in a flash by slipping favorites into clipboards and leaning on a shelf.

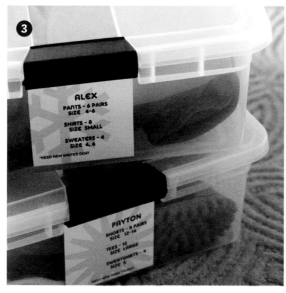

"Hang analog clocks throughout your home. Kids need to see minutes passing to understand time management, which is a big part of raising organized children."

—**Kathy Jenkins,** professional organizer

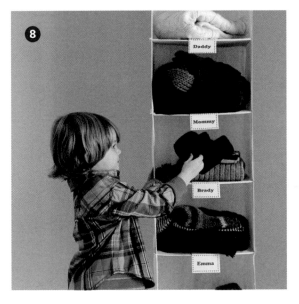

5 Place chunky and oversize books in baskets that are easy to transport from a child's bed to the family room to the backseat of your car.

6 Hide messes and boost storage by hanging a pocketed curtain panel or fabric shoe rack on a rod along the top edge of a bookcase. Drop in small stuffed animals, cars, or dolls.

7 Attach a pair of towel bars to the side of a kid's desk and use S hooks to hang pockets.

8 Place folded clothing by family member or day of the week in a hanging canvas organizer designed for adult sweaters. Add labels so everyone knows what goes where.

utility spaces

An efficient garage, laundry, basement, or mudroom is a thing of beauty. Show these hardworking spaces some love and prepare to reap rewards.

Greater productivity can be yours by asking the following questions. **How do you want to work?** Before you purchase any storage products, think about your routines. For example, how would you do laundry in an ideal world? Where do you prefer to bathe the dog? Creating a system that truly works for you is more important than any new bins or boxes. **Who else uses the space?** Every family member most likely uses your home's utility spaces. To make lasting improvements, you need to involve these people and their needs in any solution you devise. **How can you make cleaning easier?** Utility spaces get messy. Always opt for surfaces and furniture that are scrubbable.

ultimate utility room

This corridor deftly does quadruple duty as mudroom, laundry, office, and closet for cleaning supplies.

A ROLLING BENCH just inside the entrance is a comfortable place to put on shoes, which are stored in the base. A curtain masks a washer and dryer stacked in a closet.

Labels are especially important in spaces that several people use. Choose temporary labels for containers whose contents change.

Press-on letters
above right add a fun, three-dimensional flair to metal pails filled with winter accessories now and summer supplies, such as sunscreen and ball caps, later.

A flip-down bar
right offers a hanging spot for fresh-pressed garments, then lifts out of the way when ironing sessions are complete.

A storage tower
far right adjacent to the washer and dryer features a rack for ironing equipment, lazy Susans holding stain-treatment necessities, and a drawer for containers of laundry detergent.

Small pails
below right hold day-of-the-week clothespins, sewing supplies, and stain-treatment pens. The labels are created by affixing metal scrapbook letters to a length of ribbon, then gluing the ribbon to the pail.

Chalkboard tags
below, far right can be wiped clean as storage needs—and seasons—change.

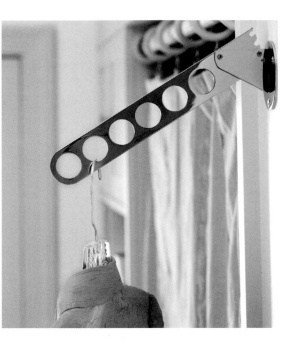

ultimate utility room

The patchwork wall *opposite* above the desk is a hardworking grid of magnet, dry-erase, cork, and pegboard squares. Patterned paper gives the corkboards personality.

Shallow compartments *above right* attached to the inside of the cleaning-supply cabinet hold categorized soaps and tools. Plastic bins inside keep brushes and sponges neat.

Recycling bins *right* reside under the desk. Rub-on labels identify contents, which can later easily be sent to the proper repository.

Hanging organizers *far right* secured to the pegboard guarantee there will always be a notepad at hand. The organizers also gather bits of important paper, such as receipts, mail, and coupons.

save time
Instead of storing all your cleaning supplies in one central place, consider placing small, room-specific kits throughout your home, such as in your bathroom, kitchen, garage, or mudroom.

in the zone

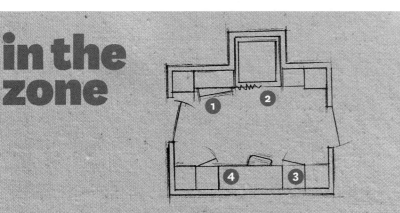

1 Built-in shelving near the door serves as a drop zone for coats, bags, and keys. A rollout bench makes tying shoes easy.

2 Stacking the washer and dryer leaves room for ironing, stain-treating, and laundry-sorting supplies.

3 Cleaning supplies tuck away inside a storage tower to the left of the desk. Even a vacuum fits inside.

4 A grid of memo boards above the desk features magnet, dry-erase, cork, and pegboard surfaces to create an organization hub.

ultimate garage

Specialized stations make it possible to not only park cars in this garage, but also squeeze in some gardening and carpentry.

SLATBOARD WALLS
spread storage options from floor to ceiling in the garage's carpentry corner. Wire baskets, hooks, bins, and shelving can be hung or repositioned in seconds.

Wall-mount plastic bins *above, far left* keep nails, screws, and other small hardware sorted by size.

A cardboard caddy *above left* steps out of the office to manage workshop gadgets and a notebook for planning.

A rolling metal cabinet *far left* is stocked with manuals, magazines, and hanging files for project notes. Magnetic clips display charts and reminders.

A towel holder *left* features a bin on top for frequently used cleaners, brushes, and safety goggles.

Specialty holders *below left* accommodate tools of various shapes and sizes. Here, loop hooks stand a battalion of screwdrivers at the ready.

Garage solutions need to stand up to heavy use. Metal and pressure-treated lumber are often your best material options.

BULBS

HUSKY
DRAWSTRING
KITCHEN
BAGS

120
BAGS

simple
green

5/25

MULCH

COMPOST
PLUS

Adjustable wire shelves *opposite* frame a wooden gardening bench, organizing seeds, tools, and pots. A memo station tracks planting schedules and watering needs. A set of rolling drawers to the right holds car-washing and other cleaning supplies.

Handled plastic bins *above right* protect seeds and other gardening provisions. Adhesive letters help identify contents.

Plastic key chains *right* stylishly label wire drawer contents.

Large plastic bins *far right* with small nesting containers sort potting materials.

save space

Your garage probably has a taller ceiling than most rooms in your home. Take advantage of that space by adding hanging storage. Look for metal racks that mount to the ceiling and feature pulley- or motor-operated lift systems.

in the zone

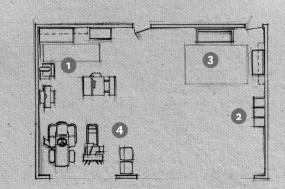

1 Slatboard and custom storage accessories on perpendicular walls hold large and small tools.

2 Recycling and trash containers sit near garage doors, out of the way but easy to roll to the curb.

3 Wire shelving and plastic bins combine to create a charming gardening center.

4 A rolling set of drawers easily moves around the garage, whether it be to wash the car or the family dog.

IES

Thrift-store finds and clever color use help this small shed bloom into charming, efficient space to nurture plants.

Garden

PEGBOARD WALLS with painted accents effectively create zones for specific types of garden tools. Cute curtains mounted below a shelf-turned-work-counter add cheerful style and practicality.

Notched cubbies *above, far left* **creatively display frequently used gardening shears on the shed's door. A thrifted bucket hangs below, corralling bug spray and citronella candles.**

Bracketed shelves *left* **across from the potting bench make space for bulky items, such as bins of specialty soil, birdseed, boots, and miniature trash cans of compost.**

Pegboard hooks *far left* **secure various gardening supplies. A sturdy canvas bag makes carrying plant food around the yard a breeze.**

Bright, retro details make this garden shed
a fun and functional place to work.

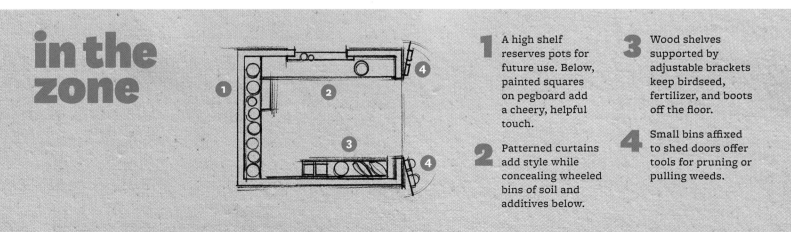

in the zone

1 A high shelf reserves pots for future use. Below, painted squares on pegboard add a cheery, helpful touch.

2 Patterned curtains add style while concealing wheeled bins of soil and additives below.

3 Wood shelves supported by adjustable brackets keep birdseed, fertilizer, and boots off the floor.

4 Small bins affixed to shed doors offer tools for pruning or pulling weeds.

essential elements

Stop outfitting your garage, basement, or laundry with cast-off furniture. These hardworking spaces require smart selections.

MOBILE SOLUTIONS

Any cabinet or worktable becomes instantly more useful when you add wheels. For maximum durability, avoid wheels that are inflatable or constructed of hard plastic or exposed metal. All casters should be heavy-duty rubber with steel ball bearings. For safety, plan to include at least two locking casters that are easy to engage with your foot. Keep everything rolling along by regularly oiling and cleaning casters to remove particles that can scrape or damage your floor.

OPEN, CONSISTENT SHELVING

Many utility rooms feature a hodgepodge of shelving. "Using one consistent type of shelving will make a big difference in feeling organized," says professional organizer Laura Leist. Choose basic, sturdy shelving in wood, engineered wood, metal, or wire. (Avoid plastic shelving because it's often brittle.) Look for generously sized shelves and compartments that can accommodate accessories such as baskets, bins, and racks from various manufacturers.

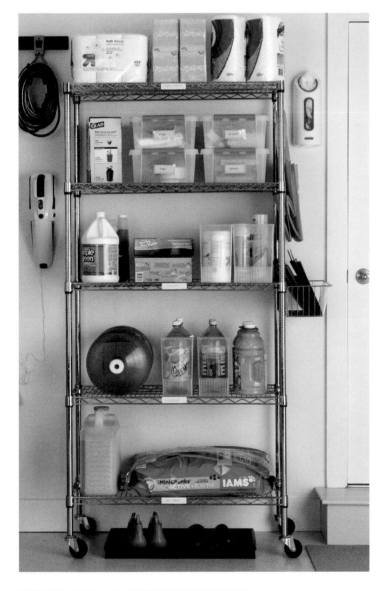

> "Pantry-style cabinets are great for wholesale club overrun. Consider adding a ready-to-assemble unit to your garage or laundry."
>
> —**Laura Leist**, professional organizer

EXPANDABLE, ADJUSTABLE SYSTEMS

Good storage systems shift to accommodate changing needs. Metal-wire/industrial-post shelving is a budget-friendly option that's adjustable. Rather than putting the entire unit together and then filling it with items, Leist recommends putting the lowest shelf in place, setting items on that shelf, and then adding the next shelf at a height that allows you to still remove the items easily. "If you add shelves one at a time, to fit around the stuff you need to store, you maximize the unit's height and storage capacity."

TOUGH WORK SURFACES

Materials matter. You want countertops and shelves that respond to quick swipes of a damp cloth or a disposable wipe, but that also stand up to rigorous scrubbing, extensive rinsing, and the occasional application of powerful cleaners. Wear and tear will happen over time, so embrace the inevitable by minimizing laminate and plastic-coated finishes and opting for metal, solid-surfacing, stone, or wood surfaces that gain a patina over years of use.

challenges | garage gear

The garage is the largest single room in many homes. Stop fearing this space and start reshaping it, bit by bit.

Garages become catchalls because they serve so many purposes. "You need to break this big space into bite-size pieces," professional organizer Laura Leist says. "Try focusing on only one area or one type of task." A gardening bench or carpentry corner, for example, is an ideal spot to make major improvements in an afternoon. Or just make one organizing decision: determining which items to let go of, or clustering items by function. "Complete one thing, even if it's small," Leist says.

Take advantage of unused vertical space with pegboard, slat board, and high-mounted shelves.

1. UP AND ROLLING
Resist the urge to dump things on the garage floor by placing gear and supply kits on wheeled shelves and carts. Come project time, simply maneuver the supplies to your work site.

2. FRESH FRONTS
Fresh semi-gloss paint and simple curtains liven up blah wood shelving. As a bonus, painted surfaces are easier than bare wood to wipe clean, and fabric panels minimize dust while concealing any clutter.

3. GREEN SMARTS
Although many cities now offer single-stream recycling, use small stacking bins to pull out items, such as batteries, lightbulbs, and building materials, that still require special disposal. A canvas bag is handy for returnable cans and bottles, while a compost pail makes the most of kitchen scraps.

4. HIGH HOLDER
Employ ceiling hooks and heavy-duty wall hangers to clear bulky bikes from the garage floor.

5. HANDY HARDWARE
Combine modular cabinets to form a station for gardening and general puttering. Hang small tools from slatted wall panels and fill clear plastic containers with seeds packets and wild animal food.

challenges | laundry

A smooth-functioning laundry is about your family's routine rather than any single product.

After you determine who's responsible for doing the laundry (parents, kids, a combination of both?), professional organizer Laura Leist recommends setting a wash schedule based on volume of clothing—for example, when the hamper is full—rather than a specific day of the week. Because laundry happens throughout your home, decide what must happen where and in what order: Where do you sort the laundry? Where to do you fold clean garments? When do you pick up clean laundry to put away?

save time
Make your entire family responsible for doing laundry. Show young kids how to pair socks and fold shirts and pants the right way. Children as young as 8 can do laundry after you teach them to sort clothing and operate appliances.

1. SHELF LIFE
Two vintage window boxes hung on their sides above a washer and dryer become a four-shelf station for organizing supplies. Putting up detergents in clear containers helps you know when you need to buy more.

2. GOT YOU PEGGED
Two pieces of metal pegboard boost the storage power of a corner. Repositionable shelves and bins hold stain treaters and scrub tools.

3. 'ROUND THE BEND
Top a front-loading washer and dryer with a counter to create a folding area. Suspend a shower curtain rod between two cabinets to wedge in a hanging area.

4. PEEK-A-BOO
Who says a laundry room has to look like a laundry room? Hide the washer and dryer behind folding doors, and fill a pullout spice cabinet with cleaners and treaters.

5. SWAP OUT
Inexpensive rubber-coated wire closet shelves top a utility zone. Swapping out a drawer for a retractable ironing board allows for quick set-up when it's time to press garments.

before & after

A homeowner creates a
clutter-free garage that satisfies
her family's storage needs.

BEFORE
problems

Molly's garage was so
sparsely furnished that
she found it difficult
to store anything
effectively. "My two
boys decided that the
middle of the floor was
a great spot for sporting
equipment, while my
husband adopted a
cluttered corner to
park the lawn mower,
snowblower, and other
machines." Though her
space wasn't necessarily
chaotic, it lacked any
systems designated
for specific tasks; as a
result, nobody bothered
to keep things tidy.

solutions

Molly and her family started by removing everything from the garage and sorting it by task, season, or activity. She then determined which storage systems best suited the things her family actually used.

1 With little interest in gardening or carpentry, Molly's family needed only a small potting/work bench created from refinished kitchen cabinetry. Metal pegboard displays hand tools, while gardening gear hangs from a closet rod.

2 Given her family's passion for sports, Molly lined two walls with a storage system that features a mix of repositionable baskets, racks, and ball holders.

3 Labels that use erasable markers make it easy to change drawer or bin contents.

4 Sturdy metal shelving is a smart solution for housing large items, such as holiday decorations, wash tubs, and coolers.

get going now

Minor changes can make a major difference in your mudroom, laundry, garage, or other hardworking space.

1 Paint silhouettes where laundry staples are supposed to go to serve as a playful reminder to put away items after you complete pressing duties.

2 Install slide-out bins in a base cabinet to collect recyclables or refuse. Dangle reusable paper bags from a bag clip mounted to the inside of the cupboard.

3 Label metal mesh rolling bins and tuck them under a shelf or worktable.

4 Affix laminated labels to sorted baskets of laundry with spray-painted clothespins. Try a similar labeling strategy on bins of folded clothing that need to return to specific rooms or family members.

"Reuse old kitchen cabinets in your garage. They're often lighter and brighter than conventional garage cabinetry."

—**Laura Leist,** professional organizer

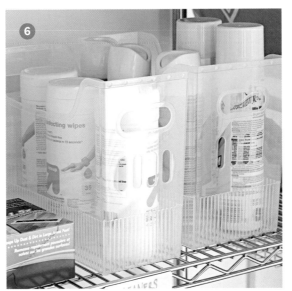

5 Keep pet shampoo and brushes stowed in a portable caddy that's easy to grab for grooming and bathing outdoors.

6 Stock up on wet wipes and other favorite cleaners. Stand slender items in plastic file bins to avoid toppling.

7 Install a wall-mount drying rack for delicate items. This version makes the most of a sliver of space under a window and folds tightly against the wall when not in use.

8 Sort rags and extra cleaning supplies in clear, labeled stacking bins. Fashion quick labels from scraps of pretty paper and clear packing tape.

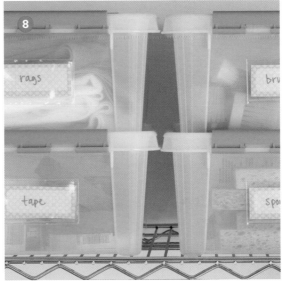

creative spaces

Hobby and crafts rooms are obvious venues for creative activity, but home offices and study spaces should be clutter-free inspiration zones, too.

Jump-start your imaginative instincts by considering the following questions. **How much do you really have?** Many people stash creative supplies in multiple rooms and are unsure of their true storage needs. Group like with like, eliminate extras, and dedicate spots to specific categories of items so you avoid overbuying. **Do you need to move it?** If you work on projects in multiple locations around or outside your home, choose sturdy containers with lids and handles for easy transport. **Do you need to see it?** Open storage helps you explore your options. Reserve tabletops, cubbies, and shelves for items you frequently mix and match, such as markers, fabric, and paper.

Clever adaptations make this spare bedroom a haven for a wide range of crafts projects.

A SIDEBOARD receives a functional makeover with a piece of laminate countertop. Additional legs support the enlarged work surface.

A pullout shelf *above left* in the bottom of a sideboard compartment is strong enough to support a sewing machine and supplies. Hooks inside the door hold scissors and measuring tools. On the countertop, a galvanized chicken feeder separates papers by color.

Wood drawer caddies *center left* prevent small crafts supplies, such as glitter and chipboard embellishments, from getting lost. Cutout handles make it easy to transport items.

A vintage toolbox *below left* is revived with a coat of spray paint and holds stamping supplies. The metal surface makes it ideal to apply a fun magnetic label.

Fabric curtains

opposite open to reveal a closet filled with ready-to-assemble storage components. Stackable cubby and drawer units store fabric and paper, while a sheet of metal pegboard corrals buttons, paper punches, scissors, and rolls of twine.

A cut-down dining table

above right partners with armchairs to host projects and snacking. A Murphy bed in cabinets along the back wall lowers to quickly shift the space from crafting space to guest room.

A magazine holder

above, far right repurposed as a yarn and knitting-supplies caddy lets you take projects anywhere.

Spools of ribbon

right on a wooden dowel inside a wall-mounted box provide easy access to an array of colorful embellishments.

A gift-wrapping station

far right is created from a folding breakfast table. The drawers on either side house bows, tape, and scissors.

in the zone

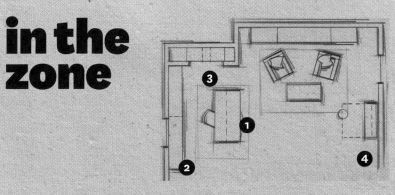

1 A generous work surface lets crafters spread out while working on projects.

2 Open shelving behind the main workspace positions frequently used supplies within arm's reach.

3 Fabric panels replace bifold doors for increased access to a closet stocked with fabric, books, and tools.

4 A gatefold table expands as a station for wrapping gifts or enjoying a snack.

small-space home office

This petite dining nook moonlights as a stylish home office with productive upgrades.

COLLECTION

PETER LINDBERGH

A MIX OF SHELVING wraps a niche in function. A modular bookcase holds client files and fabric samples, while floating shelves keep books and decor off the desk.

Labeled ribbons
above right on photo albums both identify topics and serve as bookmarks.

File boxes
above, far right stabilize glossy magazines and catalogs. Pocket labels identify titles.

An antique spring
right functions as a fun desktop holder for small notepads and planners.

Magnetic boards
far right secure inspirational images, paint chips, and fabric swatches. Wall-mount file holders below organize large binders and sketchbooks.

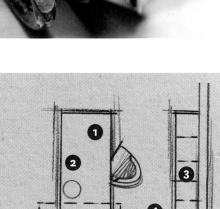

small smarts

1 A desk made of iron adds old-world charm while providing a bit of storage in three small drawers.

2 A desktop tray offers access to most-needed supplies, such as rubber bands, pencils, and tacks.

3 Gridlike shelving houses baskets and bins that store client files, inspiration books, and fabric samples.

4 Wall shelves inject extra storage. Magnetic boards and file holders keep ideas close at hand.

small-space crafts area

A forgettable basement corner is transformed into a multipurpose workspace ready for a wealth of family projects.

A CUBE-BASED modular storage system sets a clean, adaptable vibe in this corner. Shelves, dividers, drawers, and doors customize the basic units.

Acrylic pegboard *above, far left* **keeps creative supplies nearby and easy to see. Coordinating shelves, hooks, and hanging canisters corral scrapbooking supplies and specialty tools.**

Open cubbies *left* **with extra shelves sort papers, while drawers stow less-attractive items. A U-shape arrangement comfortably hosts two during study or crafting sessions.**

Magnetic boxes *below, far left* **can be reconfigured to fit in various size drawers. Here, the organizers hold stamps, stickers, and other small embellishments.**

Choose obvious, open storage solutions for items used by multiple family members.

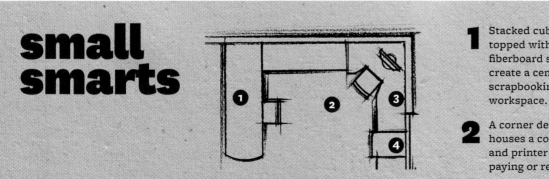

small smarts

1 Stacked cubes topped with a fiberboard slab create a centralized scrapbooking workspace.

2 A corner desk houses a computer and printer for bill-paying or research.

3 Carpet tiles attached to the wall form an unconventional board to pin key papers.

4 Near the computer, deep drawers hide file cabinets for family records.

essential elements

Enjoy that busy buzz in a room or corner set up to facilitate all forms of creative work, including crafting, writing, and studying.

FAST FILING
Papers pile up when you don't have an established filing system. Although one person or a couple may be able to manage important documents in a file box or two, consider investing in a two-drawer, letter-size file cabinet that's at least 23 inches deep and has fully extending drawers. Because a household filing system doesn't happen overnight, professional organizer Kathy Jenkins recommends setting aside one to two hours to set up your filing system and create all the labels. Then dedicate several 15-minute sessions over several weeks to sorting and filing documents.

INSPIRATION ORGANIZERS
Many creative spaces are flooded with bits of information: clippings, samples, reference books, and more. Establish one place to display your best stuff and another place to file the rest. Try clipping and saving things electronically; you probably won't miss having physical copies. "Imagine yourself in the future needing a story or a reference," Jenkins says. "Are you going to dig through your stacks of paper—or will you go online and find it again? Your preferences may already be shifting to digital storage."

"Keeping like things together is critical. Put them together—and then set up systems to keep them together."

—Kathy Jenkins, professional organizer

KITS AND CADDIES

Gather the tools and supplies required to do an activity or specific task, such as paying bills or writing thank-you cards, in a single container, which makes you edit down to the essentials and enables you to take your work anywhere. Sturdy bins and baskets with handles always work well as caddies, but gallon-size plastic freezer bags are an inexpensive alternative that display what's inside and are a snap to label with a permanent marker.

FUTURE-FOCUSED FLEXIBILITY

The tools you'll need for creative work 10—or even two—years from now are sure to be different from your current supplies. Rather than trying to predict the future, just select basic work surfaces and shelving that you can adjust easily without tools and won't mind cutting down or drilling into later on. With tomorrow in mind, stock up on square and rectangular containers with lids; they'll always sit together attractively on shelves or stack conveniently in a corner no matter what your future setup or needs are.

Paper pileup is a perennial problem for most people. Here's how to manage those stacks.

"Stop making piles and more piles," professional organizer Kathy Jenkins says. "Force yourself to respond to paper in one of four ways."

- Immediately trash or shred anything you don't need.
- Delegate any document that requires someone else's knowledge or action.
- Display papers you need to act on (unpaid bills, invitations, schedules) in an in-box or on a corkboard.
- File papers you need to keep in a box or cabinet. Use manila folders—handwritten labels are just fine—and hanging files.

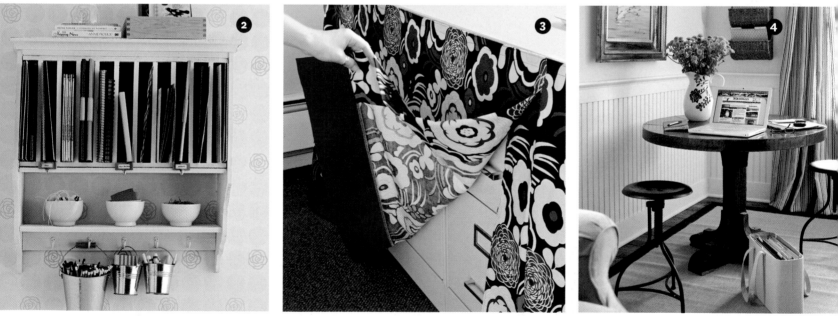

Always write or print your own file labels. Preprinted label kits are available, but your filing needs are unique.

1. BOXED BEAUTIES

Open boxes or bins are useful to group papers and other items for specific active projects. When it's time to archive, edit down to only the documents you need to retain and shift them to a sturdy lidded banker's box.

2. DISH IT OUT

File papers, magazines, and notebooks in a wood plate rack, using labels attached to the cabinet frame to guide sorting.

3. COVER UP

Tack a short curtain to the top edge of a series of file cabinets to give them a quick facelift.

4. PORTABLE PAPERS

A canvas file box with handles and a set of wall-mount pockets transform a breakfast nook into a mini office.

5. SAVVY STATION

Combine tools that let you easily act on, delegate, trash, or file every piece of paper that comes your way. Here, a three-tray in-box sorts papers by required actions. Bulletin boards dedicated to the current week or one person target specific deadlines or family members.

Put your coolest tools on display to boost your productivity and get a great-looking work space.

Successfully storing office and crafts supplies is more about ongoing inventory control than purchasing specialized containers. "You don't know how much you really have until you bring it all together, " professional organizer Kathy Jenkins says. You'll make better decisions about what to keep and what to get rid of when you see everything in one location. "And whenever you bring in a new item, store like with like—and ruthlessly evaluate which items you truly need to keep," Jenkins says.

1. TRAY CHIC

Don't toss office supplies in a drawer. A tray, a wire glass holder, and a mix of white ceramic glassware can be used to show off pens, pencils, and odds and ends.

2. CAN-DO CANISTERS

Cover soup cans in scraps of pretty paper and link them together with hot glue to fashion modular desk storage. Avoid clutter by dedicating each opening to a specific stationery staple.

3. THAT'S A WRAP

Papers and ribbons are too pretty to roll up and stow away. Slide tension rods through your favorites and suspend inside an open cabinet compartment.

4. HEAVENLY METAL

Adhere magnetic spice tins, memo clips, and pencil holders to the interior and exterior of a metal bin for a go-anywhere supply source.

5. PEGBOARD CHIC

Pegboard above a workstation in a crafts room or office offers flexible hanging storage for tools, trims, and other necessities. A repurposed mailbox holds tags and cradles a roll of paper.

When a dedicated room isn't possible, make the most of slivers of space with these unconventional ideas.

Most homes can squeeze in a special spot for crafting or studying; all it takes is a little ingenuity. Stand in the middle of each room and consider the untapped space in corners, below windows, under eaves, and behind doors. Stack cube-based storage components in unusually shaped areas, maximizing every bit of volume. Chairs, carts, and other wheeled furnishings are easy to roll into the space during work time and move later to free up floor space for other activities.

5

1. OFFICE IN A BOX

A wall-hugging cupboard opens to reveal office supplies. Covering the inside of the doors with chalkboard paint lets you leave reminders. Below, a shelf fitted with glass cups tends pencils, pens, and scissors.

2. TRY ANGLE

Stack cabinet boxes and wall cubbies to work with slanted ceilings in a top-floor room.

3. CRAFTY CLOSET

Attach a pegboard to the inside of a door and hang shelves, paint tubes, and specialty scissors. A wheeled dresser and suitcase transition from room to room.

4. MOVABLE ART

Adhering corkboard to the inside of a kitchen island cabinet introduces space to hang sketches and notes. The casters allow you relocate the station to capture the best natural light for drawing or painting.

5. OFFICE SPACE

Use table legs and wall brackets to convert a prefinished wall shelf into a slim desk within a closet. Add paint, a pendant light, bulletin boards, and various ready-to-assemble storage units to complete the transformation.

before & after

A family refines their home office, instituting smart storage that works for everyone.

BEFORE
problems

With two jobs and three active children, Wendy and Todd found their basement office had become less of a work space and more of a dumping ground for old paperwork, sports equipment, and kids' crafts. The space was so chaotic, in fact, that the busy family often found themselves working at the kitchen table, ignoring the growing piles downstairs.

AFTER
solutions

The first task professional organizer Laurie Leist had the couple complete was a thorough editing of items in the office. The entire family got into the process. The kids shredded old paperwork, Todd moved sports equipment to a storage room, and Wendy sorted household documents into labeled folders. "I learned that you don't need to keep every piece of paper or artwork," Wendy says. "We realized less is more."

1 A wheeled file cabinet stores essential household documents and pulls out as a bonus work surface.

2 Thousands of digital images that were previously stored on cameras and memory cards were archived onto compact discs, which were then filed into labeled three-ring binders for easy referral.

3 Artwork that Wendy and Todd decided to save went into portfolios labeled with each child's name.

4 School supplies that everyone can use shifted to patterned boxes on an easy-to-reach shelf. Below the boxes, each child's art portfolio is labeled in their own handwriting.

get going now

Better manage your creative resources in your home office and crafts room with these quick upgrades.

1 Stand files you use on a daily or weekly basis in a dish-drying rack. The silverware bucket efficiently sorts pencils, pens, and notepads.

2 Toss thread, buttons, and other small accessories into glass candy jars and display on open shelves.

3 Affix a roll of crafts paper to the underside of a table for an instant drawing zone.

4 Repurpose a hanging jewelry organizer with see-through pouches to hold frequently used crafting items. Dangle it from a nail near your work surface and then hang it in a closet when you're done working on a project.

Create an inventory of items stored out of sight on a note card you tape to the lid of a box or inside a cabinet door.

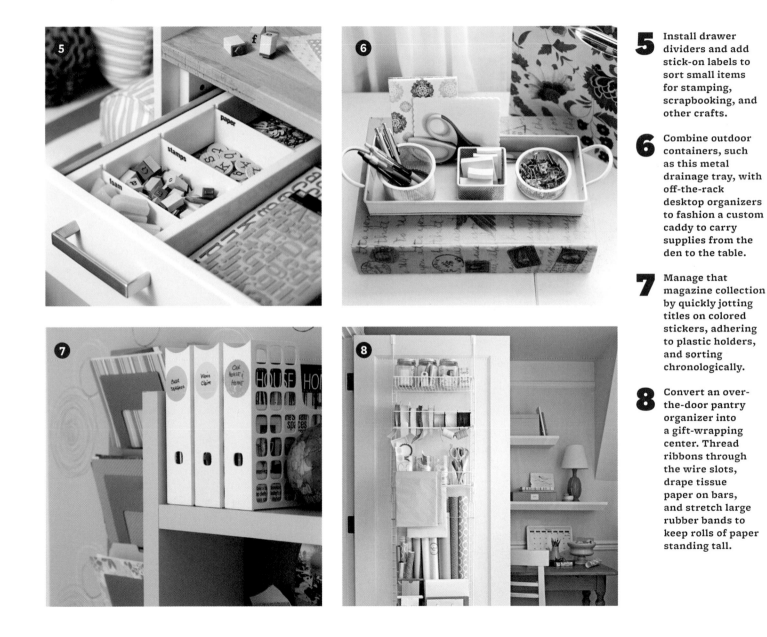

5 Install drawer dividers and add stick-on labels to sort small items for stamping, scrapbooking, and other crafts.

6 Combine outdoor containers, such as this metal drainage tray, with off-the-rack desktop organizers to fashion a custom caddy to carry supplies from the den to the table.

7 Manage that magazine collection by quickly jotting titles on colored stickers, adhering to plastic holders, and sorting chronologically.

8 Convert an over-the-door pantry organizer into a gift-wrapping center. Thread ribbons through the wire slots, drape tissue paper on bars, and stretch large rubber bands to keep rolls of paper standing tall.

workroom

Roll up your sleeves and start tackling the nitty-gritty of getting organized. Our expert advice on choosing containers, making labels, outfitting cabinets, and upgrading closets will guide you every step along the way.

choosing containers | by material

Simply put: Materials matter. A container's composition significantly affects its performance, so rely on these tips to match container material to desired function.

1 **Acrylic** shows off what's inside, so plan to fill these containers with attractive items or things you need to identify instantly. Because it scratches easily, acrylic may not be suited for heavy kitchen or bath use.

2 **Bamboo and teak** are tight-grained and water-resistant, making them appropriate for moist environments.

3 **Wire** ranges from lightweight and inexpensive to sturdy and pricey. Plastic and rubber coatings add durability and functionality in wet environments. Wire mesh is a good option for holding small items.

4 **Wood** is a hardy option that can be painted or stained for various looks. Look for solid construction at the corners.

5 **Fabric and canvas** can inject color and pattern quickly and often inexpensively. Choose cloth that you can wipe clean or launder.

6 **Woven materials** allow air to circulate. The typical soft-side construction is ideal for storing kids' stuff.

7 **Vinyl** can be clear or opaque. It wipes clean easily and is best for lightweight items.

8 **Cardboard and pressboard** are often painted or wrapped in paper. Check lid and corner construction because these parts usually tear first.

9 **Leather** is durable and handsome. Plan to polish and care for these containers as you would a pair of good shoes. Avoid using in moist environments.

10 **Metal** is tough, protective, and often heavy. Seek out hardy finishes that stand up to scratches and scrubbing while shrugging off tarnish and rust.

11 **Plastic** is available in an ever-expanding range of colors and transparencies. It's your go-to choice for items that may drip or leak, or when you need an airtight seal.

12 **Natural fibers** can be stained, painted, or left natural. Many are eco-friendly and durable. Popular options include straw, wicker, willow, rattan, rush, and pandan.

choosing containers | by shape

A good-looking container becomes a favorite when its shape perfectly suits your storage needs. Pay attention to the pros and cons of the most common options on the market today.

1 Bins are ideal for stuff you interact with often, but they don't protect contents from dust or moisture.

2 Caddies feature handles and dividers for organizing smaller items. Designed for flatware and tools, they repurpose well in baths, offices, and playrooms.

3 Buckets are often meant to be decorative rather than hardworking, so test handle and container strength in the store. Tapered sides means you sacrifice some storage space.

4 Nesting containers come in graduated sets of two to five pieces or more. They look substantial when displayed and are helpful for sorting, but accessing an individual container can be a challenge when the set is stacked.

5 Specialty carriers abound for crafts and office gear, especially items that move between locations. They're often worth the extra price because they offer protective, perfectly scaled storage.

6 Canisters look great displayed on shelves and counters, but you sacrifice significant storage space due to their cylindrical shape.

7 Boxes, because of their lids, are best for holding items you access less frequently. Shop for sturdy versions that allow for stacking. Plan to add labels.

8 Baskets can be filled attractively to the brim with linens, crafts supplies, or toys. They don't stack well, but handled versions are convenient to transport.

9 Trays are shallow and ideal for stashing papers, utensils, office supplies, toiletries, and other small items. Look for versions with lips at least 2 inches tall to secure contents.

10 Stacking containers save space on shelves and desktops. Plan to add labels to container exteriors so you know what's stored at each level without having to disassemble the entire stack.

choosing containers | kitchen

When effectively implemented, organizers for cooking spaces and food storage cut kitchen clutter. Stock up on these culinary essentials.

Wine racks

What they're best for
Protecting and safely stacking bottled beverages inside a cabinet, on a shelf, or on the floor.

What to look for
Seek out sturdy compartments that cradle each bottle and minimize rattling. Test with a variety of bottle shapes and sizes so you know your favorites will fit. If the rack will be in the open, splurge on a stylish version.

Cautions
Decorative racks are generally stand-alone, so if you need to store more bottles, invest in an expandable system.

Unconventional uses
Fill with rolled hand towels in a guest bath. Turn on its side and place in a drawer as a divider for glassware.

Utensil trays

What they're best for
Sorting essential implements for eating and cooking.

What to look for
At least one side should adjust so you can tailor the size to better fit a drawer's dimensions. Opt for materials that are easy to wipe clean or place in the dishwasher. A modular system with interlinking compartments may be best if you're storing unusual-shape items.

Cautions
Felt- and velvet-covered trays are lovely but best reserved for fine silver you use rarely.

Unconventional uses
Sort tea packets and other single-serve beverage mixes. Organize candles, matches, and lighters in a utility drawer.

Quilted

What they're best for
Safeguarding china and other breakables that you use infrequently.

What to look for
Coordinated sets accommodate a wide range of dish and glassware sizes. Choose containers that hold your dishes snugly—but not tightly.

Cautions
Quilted containers alone won't protect items inside from rattling against one another. Plan to add thin sheets of foam or felt between plates; use dividers for cups and stemware.

Unconventional uses
Pack precious holiday ornaments in containers designed for teacups or stemware. Stuff with off-season gear (one type of garment in each container) and stack on a high shelf until next season.

Spice storage

What they're best for
Keeping favorite flavors fresh and at the ready.

What to look for
You want containers that are airtight, so look for rubber or plastic seals. A reusable, expandable system can evolve as your needs change. Basic lidded cylinders are more versatile than cleverly shaped containers.

Cautions
Prefilled spice racks rarely offer fresh-enough seasonings. Empty and refill with the spices you actually like and use.

Unconventional uses
Separate sewing notions or miscellaneous hardware in repair kits. Repurpose a rack as an office supply holder or display for a collection.

Plastic bags

What they're best for
Packing leftovers and lunchables in a handy, airtight manner.

What to look for
Plastic bags come in a range of sizes and qualities, but generally you get what you pay for. Gusseted corners let you stuff bags to their max. Double- and triple-zipper tops supply a strong seal.

Cautions
If you reuse plastic bags, wash thoroughly with soap and water and allow to fully air-dry.

Unconventional uses
Oh, what you can do with them! Organize the contents of a purse or other bag with clustered essentials. Gather travel toiletries in a single safe spot. Hang on a bulletin board as a see-through pouch for mail or coupons.

Specialty & novelty

What they're best for
Providing specialized protection to specific food items.

What to look for
Pick products that help you store foods you use several times a week (lunch-packing helpers) or only in small portions (produce, sauces).

Cautions
Some specialty products are very poorly made. Good materials and solid construction must accompany clever design. Rigorously test before purchasing and ask yourself if you already have a general-purpose container that does a good enough job.

Unconventional uses
Organize the interior of a toolbox. Use as mini kits for first-aid or manicure supplies.

Plastic

What they're best for
Storing food in the refrigerator, freezer, or pantry.

What to look for
Tight-fitting lids are a must, and lids that work on multiple-size containers are a plus. The main material should be dishwasher-safe, BPA-free, and stain-resistant. Clear containers let you skip labels.

Cautions
Skip inexpensive plastic containers altogether; they usually warp in the dishwasher and take on stains. Avoid heating or reheating plastic containers.

Unconventional uses
Classify small accessories and jewelry. Drill a few holes in the bottom and use in the bath or shower to corral shampoos and scrubs.

Disposable

What they're best for
Sending leftovers home with guests after a party or big meal.

What to look for
Several manufacturers now make disposable plasticware. Pick the system you prefer and stock up, so your sizes and shapes are consistent.

Cautions
Most lids fit loosely. Add a layer of plastic wrap if you're concerned about spills, or seek out containers with screw-top lids. Avoid heating or reheating plastic containers.

Unconventional uses
Store paint or stain overnight while working on a project. Transport delicate items such as fancy cupcakes or cut flowers.

Glass

What they're best for
Storing foods you want to reheat.

What to look for
Start with a nesting set of three to five glassware pieces in graduated sizes. Purchase more of the sizes you use most. Lids should be tight-fitting; venting options are important if the lids are microwavable.

Cautions
Know what your glassware is capable of. Double-check whether lids are microwavable; some aren't. Verify that containers can go from freezer to microwave without cracking.

Unconventional uses
Fill a large container with a mix of sandwich-making supplies. Marinate meats and veggies, then scrub container thoroughly.

Vacuum-sealed

What they're best for
Guarding dry goods from moisture or pests.

What to look for
The vacuum-sealing mechanism needs to be easy to operate and must create an instant airtight seal.

Cautions
Avoid systems that require an additional tool or pump to fully remove air. You want to be able to fill, seal, and move on. Also, most vacuum-sealed containers are acrylic, not plastic, so plan to hand-wash them.

Unconventional uses
Keep extra cedar blocks and sachets fresh until you need them. Minimize strong scents of oils and soaps in a linen closet.

choosing containers | office

A clutter-free office requires specialty products to stop paper pileup and tame pesky office supplies. Here's what you need to know before you buy.

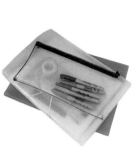

Hanging folders

What they're best for
Classifying and sequencing documents.

What to look for
Choose between letter- or legal-size and then purchase several boxes of basic manila folders and a box of single-color hanging files. If you like to color code, add other solid-color hanging folders for each major topic: Financial, Insurance, Autos, Personal, and Home.

Cautions
Trendy printed hanging files result in a cluttered-looking cabinet. Plus, you usually can't find the same design when you need to expand.

Unconventional uses
Sort a pile of photos or inspiration images. Organize a collection of clutch purses and billfolds.

Magazine holders

What they're best for
Standing up periodicals and other papers.

What to look for
Choose holders that remain steady even when full. Plan to purchase several, plus a few extras. Your collection is sure to grow, and you'll want a consistent look later on.

Cautions
Avoid holders with large holes or slits; they tend to snag or crumple magazines during use.

Unconventional uses
Create an outdoor dining caddy with paper plates, napkins, and plastic cutlery. Lay holders on their side and position in a corner; use to file incoming papers or frequently used forms.

Pouches & envelopes

What they're best for
Transporting small clusters of important papers or favorite supplies.

What to look for
Clear vinyl or plastic shows off contents. You want to have a mix of sizes on hand. Test corners and zippers.

Cautions
Snap closures are fine for envelopes that hold papers only, but choose a zippered pouch when storing smaller items. Multiple plastic envelopes tend to slide around; bind together with a large binder clip or rubber band.

Unconventional uses
Replace the box a puzzle or game came in with a large pouch. Drop in a purse as a see-through cosmetics case.

Photo boxes

What they're best for
Containing piles of pictures in lieu of a photo album.

What to look for
Corners reinforced with metal make for a more durable box. Precut cardboard section dividers are easy to label yourself and use to sort between major categories such as Family, Friends, Pets, Travel, and Sports.

Cautions
Inexpensive boxes are rarely 100% acid-free. (Acids discolor photos over time.) If you're concerned, invest in good-quality boxes.

Unconventional uses
Combine tools and supplies for specific projects, such as wall repair, picture hanging, and shoe care. Ditch the lid and cluster DVDs or CDs by topic.

Media boxes

What they're best for
Compiling mismatched printed items.

What to look for
Seek out boxes sized to support letter-size hanging folders, so you can store files and loose papers in a single spot. An attached lid facilitates transport and stacking.

Cautions
A poorly managed media box can quickly turn into a dumping ground. Plan to review the contents monthly and eliminate obsolete material.

Unconventional uses
Archive a single school year or specific project in one box. Establish a portable library of children's books that can travel from bedside to living room to the back seat of your car.

Pencil cups

What they're best for
Clustering writing implements, rulers, scissors, and other office accoutrements.

What to look for
A cup that coordinates with your other desk accessories makes your work space look more organized. Because the bottom of the cup is often messy, choose a washable material.

Cautions
While one huge cup may seem appealing, you often end up with a heavy container that masks some tools. Go with two or more smaller cups instead.

Unconventional uses
Drop in brushes and other hair-care tools on your vanity. Present a handful of mixed silverware on a casual dining table.

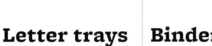

Letter trays

What they're best for
Providing a visual reminder of important documents you need to take action on.

What to look for
Your organizer needs at least three trays, one for each common response you have to paper: Pay, Respond, and File. Removable trays let you take a pile to another work space.

Cautions
A shallow tray is better than a deep one because it forces you to review contents more frequently.

Unconventional uses
Set out jewelry and other accessories for three future outfits. Sort cloth napkins in a linen cabinet.

Binders

What they're best for
Grouping together papers on a single topic or for a presentation.

What to look for
Plastic or vinyl-coated pressboard are the hardest-wearing materials. Make certain that the ring mechanisms operate easily and close firmly.

Cautions
Spend less time creating and maintaining your binders by purchasing clear vinyl sheet covers in various orientations, which better protect documents and let you skip the three-hole punch.

Unconventional uses
Outfit with vinyl inserts sized for discs and create a DVD binder. Organize recipes clipped from magazines and printed from websites into a cookbook.

Mini drawers

What they're best for
Holding small items on a desktop or in a cabinet.

What to look for
A unit with several sizes of drawers gives you options. Clear acrylic is good if you want to find things fast. Make sure all pieces glide smoothly.

Cautions
Drawers place a barrier between you and the items they contain, so be wary of placing drawers in inconvenient places that require even more effort on your part.

Unconventional uses
Establish personal drop boxes in an entry for each family member's keys and wallets. Teach a child organizing early, using mini drawers to sort hair accessories, action figures, or collections.

Drawer trays

What they're best for
Taming desk drawers.

What to look for
Wood, plastic, acrylic, and metal mesh systems are all available. Select one with a mix of compartment sizes that suits your needs. Look for tabs and magnets to link together individual trays.

Cautions
Trays tend to slide around. Line drawers with rubberized vinyl to keep things in place.

Unconventional uses
Secure several bottles of dressing or condiments in the refrigerator; they're easier to transport to the table, and you'll catch drips. Roll ties or belts and place inside by color.

choosing labels

adhesive labels

The variety of adhesive labels available today can be overwhelming. Although the designs, shapes, and fonts keep changing, the following basic strategies hold true:

Look for labels. Of course, office supply stores, discount retailers, and stationery shops have lots of options, but don't miss the good stuff at hardware stores, groceries, gardening centers, and toy stores.

Stand up to water and cold. Most adhesive labels work best on dry surfaces at room temperature, but at hardware stores and home centers, you can find some designed for extreme conditions. You'll find freezer labels alongside food storage containers.

Handwritten is just fine. Printed labels look great, but so do hand-lettered ones. Always write the label before applying it. If your label is small or an unusual size, trace the shape on a scrap piece of paper and practice writing your text. Most important: Keep going! Most handwriting looks terrible when you stop in the middle of a word or phrase.

THERE'S THE RUB
Look online for premade vinyl words that you transfer by rubbing and then peeling away the plastic backing.

LANDING SPOTS
Affix adhesive labels to the sides and bottoms of trays to assign a specific destination for every item.

ROUND WRAPPERS
Handwritten labels add a final touch to pantry goods. Ensure freshness by noting when items were canned.

LETTER BY LETTER
Assemble words and short phrases with letter stickers. Lightly draw a pencil line to keep your label level; erase when done.

tags & tied-on labels

For less-structured labeling, tie on a tag. As a bonus, you don't have to worry about a sticker peeling off. Keep the following in mind:

Heavier is better. Nonadhesive labels hold up to use best when printed on heavy cardstock, cardboard, or wood. Laminate paper labels to boost durability. Take your labels to a copy center to be laminated, or purchase a home laminating machine.

Connections matter. Ribbon and string are the standard connectors between tags and containers, but rubber bands, hair ties, lightweight chain, wire, and zip ties can all do the job as well.

Be two-faced. Most tags are secured in only one spot, so they move freely. If your hang tags are frequently flipping over, label both sides of the tag so your message is always clear.

Color-coding adds an extra layer of organizing to any labeling project. Try assigning one color to a specific task, family member, or topic.

CRAFTY CONNECTION
Drill holes in wood or pressboard shapes. After you add paint and lettering, tie onto containers as hanging tags.

KEYED IN
Write your own words on the back of the paper insert on a key ring or luggage tag. Then slip the ring onto your container.

HAPPENING HARDWARE
Thread ribbon through a metal-rim key tag and add a round sticker label. Tie onto basket handles.

STICKY FIX
Use a few inches of tape to loop around wire shelving. Leave some tape in your loop exposed so it can stick to the tag.

choosing labels

other labeling ideas

The options and opportunities for innovative, informative labels are nearly endless. Remember these concepts as you try out new products and come up with your own ideas.

Keep it simple. Elaborate labels can look great, but the best real-world labels must be easy—easy to create and revise, attach and remove. Labeling should be a way to solidify the organizing changes you make, rather than a contest to craft up the cutest tag.

Let the container guide you. A container's shape or material can lead you to specific types of labels. For instance, woven surfaces offer lots of options for attaching labels, while clear containers can be labeled from inside, creating a seamless exterior surface.

Test first. Paint pens, dry-erase markers, and grease pencils all leave marks on a variety of surfaces, including glass, ceramic, plastic, acrylic, mirror, and metal. Some combinations can be wiped clean—great for containers with ever-changing contents—while others are permanent. Try out any combination in an inconspicuous place such as the container bottom to ensure that its properties suit your labeling needs.

CLIP CHAMP
Combine colorful clips and scraps of paper to create impromptu labels for bins and baskets.

METAL MAGIC
Make the most of metal by adding magnetic letters or tags with magnets glued to the back.

WRITE ON/WIPE OFF
Cover small wood plaques or entire container exteriors with chalkboard paint, now available in an array of colors.

PICTO-PANACHE
Snap a photo of each family member, slide it into a plastic name tag holder, and attach to a bin for each person's stuff.

your labeling toolkit

You don't want anything to take you out of the moment of getting organized, including the process of making labels. Gather some basic tools and versatile supplies in a caddy (this one was designed for silverware), and start whipping up fab labels fast.

save money

Stop purchasing duplicate items. Create a bulleted inventory of a storage tub's contents with a marker and sheet of paper. Secure the list with packing tape to the container's lid or side.

Stock your kit with these essential supplies:

1 **Adhesive letters** combine to form words and short phrases.

2 **Adhesive labels** are great for flat, clean surfaces. Purchase a mix of sizes and shapes that are easy to write on.

3 **Scissors** let you trim tags and strings in a snap.

4 **Fine-point permanent markers** work on a range of surfaces. Include several colors to allow for color-coding.

5 **Pre-cut tags** just require your text to become custom hanging labels.

6 **Cotton string** secures tags to containers.

7 **Metal-rimmed key tags** link onto handles and woven surfaces.

8 **An electronic label maker** churns out printed adhesive labels with the touch of a button or two.

9 **A hole punch** makes hanging tags possible.

maximizing cabinet interiors

Whether your built-ins are custom, stock, or original to your home, boost their function by installing these add-ons.

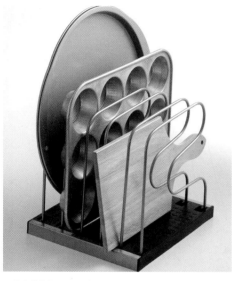

RACKS
Wire dividers let you stand pans, cutting boards, lids, and platters on their sides. Some racks are secured inside the cabinet, while others simply sit on the base.

PULLOUT SHELVES
Reach easily all the way to the back of a cabinet by replacing fixed shelves with shallow trays on rollers. Look for kits that mount to cabinet sides and bottoms.

LAZY SUSANS
Tame voluminous spaces and tricky corners with these rotating wonders. Look for light-yet-tough versions with high-impact plastic shelves and ball-bearing hardware.

OVER-THE-DOOR SOLUTIONS
Hook a door-hugging basket or bar to a cabinet door without using a single tool. Display the organizer if you want instant access, or hide inside the cabinet for less-lovely items.

PULLOUT BINS
Introduce layers of storage within a cabinet box by adding a series of bins or drawers. The functional gains far outweigh the space you sacrifice to the freestanding frame.

INSERTS
Available in a wide range of prices and styles, these specialty organizers help manage your tricky stuff: pots and pans, heavy items, small appliances, and more.

Finding the best cabinet inserts and add-ons

A hardworking cabinet usually requires a mix of organizing products. Many options are available at discount stores and home centers, but you can also find great specialty solutions from these retailers and manufacturers:

Azar
azardisplays.com
DrawerDecor
drawerdecor.com
Hafele
hafele.com
Kitchen Source
kitchensource.com
Rev-a-Shelf
rev-a-shelf.com
Simplehuman
simplehuman.com
Shelf Genie
shelfgenie.com

Never assume that two cabinets in the same room have identical dimensions. Take thorough measurements of the interiors of each and every cabinet you plan to upgrade. Realize that cabinets are rarely perfectly square, so measure all sides and plan to use shims, washers, and other spacing devices to compensate for variations.

making over a closet

Common closet conundrums

Any of these pesky closet problems look familiar? Rest assured that there's hope for your chaotic closet if it includes any (or all!) of the following:

1 Non-clothing items, such as extra housewares and old electronics, stashed on upper shelves.

2 Tall stacks of folded clothing that are certain to tumble at any moment.

3 Long-term-storage items, such as a wedding dress or special baby clothes, taking up space you use daily.

4 A single rod loaded with a mix of hangers, including the dreaded wire version from your dry cleaner.

5 A jumble of hanging garments, not sorted by type or length.

6 Sliding doors or any restriction that blocks you from seeing your entire closet at once.

7 Stacked, unlabeled boxes filled with shoes (presumably).

8 Failed organizing products, such as this unused wire shoe holder.

Long hanging, short hanging, shelves, and bins—
your closet's exact mix of components must match
your wardrobe, daily routine, and storage style.

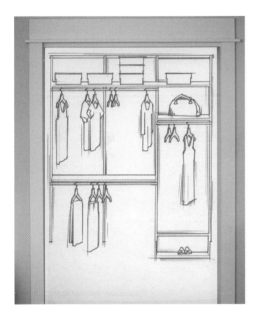

If you prefer to hang your clothes

PLAN TO:
- Inventory your shirts, pants, skirts, dresses, and coats.
- Allot as much horizontal space as possible to rods for short and long hanging.
- Double-hang a section of rods to store more shirts and skirts.
- Keep shoes in hanging organizers or on the floor.

INVEST IN:
- Epoxy-coated steel rods and shelves.
- Flocked hangers so clothing stays put.
- Specialty hangers for pants and skirts.

If you prefer to fold your clothes

PLAN TO:
- Install as many shelves as possible; dedicate pullout bins to smaller items.
- Group shelves in sections, so they function like open dressers.
- Limit stacks to 12 inches high to prevent toppling.
- Leave at least 6 inches between the top of a stack and the shelf above for easier access.

INVEST IN:
- Ventilated shelves to encourage airflow.
- 12-inch-deep shelves to hold folded sweaters and bulkier items.

If you have lots of shoes and accessories

PLAN TO:
- Include enough cubbies or angled shelves to house every pair you wear in season.
- Box up off-season and special-occasion items; label and store on high shelves.
- Outfit drawers with divided organizers for accessories.

INVEST IN:
- Laminate or wood systems for cubbies, shelves, and drawers.
- Velvet-lined trays for jewelry.
- Specialty holders for belts, ties, and more.

selecting a closet system

One system does not fit all when it comes to closets. Consider the three major categories and then explore the options that best fit your budget.

wire

Wall brackets support vinyl-coated wire shelves, hang bars, and other components.

PROS:
- Reasonable price.
- Several lines available at major retailers and home centers.
- More accessories and add-ons appearing every year.
- Can add elements as your budget allows.

CONS:
- Installing yourself requires some basic tools and skills.
- Most systems are difficult to install alone.
- Open shelves can let items fall through or can leave impressions on folded clothing.
- Sizing and hardware vary among systems.

modular

Ready-to-assemble units stack and combine to fill your space.

PROS:
- Components gain strength and stability as you combine units.
- Several lines available at major retailers and home centers.
- More specialty organizers and components appearing every year.
- Can add elements as your budget allows.
- Easier to install alone.

CONS:
- Assembling yourself requires time and some basic tools.
- Challenging to combine different systems.
- Cost of specialty components adds up quickly.

professionally installed

Closet components are custom sized and designed to fit your space and needs, then installed in your home.

PROS:
- Components perfectly match your closet's dimensions and specific storage needs.
- Can select from a wider range of finishes and hardware options, enabling you to match your decor.
- Professional design consultations can help you plan your space better.

CONS:
- Longer lead time.
- Higher price.

system	type	how to find	contact
CALIFORNIA CLOSETS	Professionally installed modular systems. Finishes range from white laminate to Italian wood veneers.	Approximately 100 franchise locations worldwide.	888/336-9707; *californiaclosets.com*
CLOSET FACTORY	Professionally installed custom-designed systems. Melamine and solid-wood finishes available.	82 franchise locations worldwide.	800/634-9000; *closetfactory.com*
CLOSETS BY DESIGN	Professionally installed modular system at three price points.	Locations nationwide.	888/500-9215; *closetsbydesign.com*
CLOSETMAID	Wire shelving. Easy-to-install vertical standards combine with an array of brackets, bars, and shelves.	Sold at retailers nationwide.	800/874-0008; *closetmaid.com*
THE CONTAINER STORE	Steel wire components (elfa), as well as components in an array of wood finishes (elfa decor).	Sold online and through 48 stores nationwide; free design service in stores, by phone, and online.	888/266-8246; *containerstore.com*
EASY TRACK/ORG	Modular ready-to-assemble components (Easy Track); professionally installed line (ORG).	Easy Track sold at retail and home center stores or online; ORG available through authorized dealers.	800/562-4257; *easytrack.com*, *homeorg.com*
EASYCLOSETS.COM	Modular components in seven colors; numerous upgrades and accessories.	Sold exclusively online; design online or use free design service. Customer services by phone.	800/910-0129; *easyclosets.com*
JOHN LOUIS HOME	Solid-wood modular components in multiple finishes.	Sold online at retailers and through specialty stores, home centers, and authorized dealers.	800/480-6985; *johnlouishome.com*
POLIFORM USA	Modular components custom-designed to fit your space.	Available through corporate showrooms and dealers nationwide.	888/765-4367; *poliformusa.com*
RUBBERMAID	Wire shelving, plus baskets, drawers, and other accessories.	Available online and at home centers.	888/895-2110; *rubbermaid.com*
SCHULTE STORAGE	Modular components in six finishes.	Available online.	513/277-3700; *schultestorage.com*, *freedomrail.com*
STUDIO BECKER	Professionally installed custom-made components.	Sold through authorized dealers and showrooms worldwide.	510/865-1616; *studiobecker.com*
WOODTRAC BY SAUDER	Modular components in three finishes.	Available online and through dealers nationwide. Professional installation available.	855/854-7465; *woodtrac.com*

installing closet components

Whether you're doing the work yourself to save money or you just enjoy home improvement projects, you can install most closet systems by yourself. Follow these tips for best results.

Start fresh. You can't effectively make over a closet with clothing in it. Remove all items and old shelving and rods. Repair walls and then paint or paper for a clean look. Upgrade lighting with LED bulbs or a new ceiling fixture. Consider replacing sliding doors with bifold doors, pocket doors, or curtains, which give you access to your entire closet at once.

Edit, sort—then shop. To purchase the right types and numbers of closet components, you must review all your clothing—discarding or donating damaged, ill-fitting, and unused items. (*See page 20* for help with editing.) Sort the remaining items by type, and inventory the garments your closet needs to store.

Plan for new acquisitions. "One in, one out" is the ideal when it comes to adding clothes to your closet, but cut yourself some slack and purchase components that will accommodate 10 to 20 percent growth over time.

save time
Online design tools—we used the website for elfa shelving from The Container Store—let you combine closet components and double-check that you have everything you need before installing.

1. MEASURE YOUR CLOSET & PLAN
Note all relevant dimensions, including door swing and light placement. See *page 29* for more about measuring. Use paper or online tools to plan out the design of your new closet and then purchase the necessary components

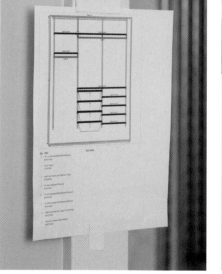

2. POST YOUR PLAN
Before you begin installing, tape your layout to a door frame or nearby wall. Unwrap all materials.

3. HANG THE HIGHEST ELEMENT
Use a level to place the top track or rack, depending on your system. Use anchors for holes that don't line up with studs.

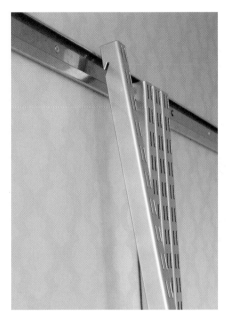

4. HANG VERTICAL ELEMENTS

Link standards to the top piece. With elfa systems, the standards simply hook onto the track; others require hardware.

5. ATTACH SHELF BRACKETS

Cluster standards together as you install brackets to keep them at the same level, then spread out standards per directions.

6. INSTALL SHELVES

Hang smallest, shallowest shelves first, then work on longer and deeper ones. Be sure shelves lock into brackets.

7. ADJUST SHELVES

If you need to reposition shelves, start from the lowest shelf, allowing for adequate clearance at each level.

Working with wire shelving

The elfa closet system shown on *pages 252–255* requires only a few tools: a drill, screwdriver, level, measuring tape, and rubber mallet. If you're installing rubber-coated wire shelving (available at most home centers and through several manufacturers), keep the following in mind.

Wire shelving comes in two gauges. "Closet gauge" works fine for most clothing closets. Reserve the more expensive "heavy gauge" components for your garage.

Cut with care. If your home center or hardware store won't cut wire shelving for a small fee, you'll need to use a bolt cutter or a hacksaw with an appropriate blade.

Cut it short. Trim shelves and other horizontal elements a half-inch shorter than the space they need to fit. The slightly smaller pieces are easier to fit into end brackets without scratching surrounding walls.

Make it secure. Don't skimp on the wall clips and angled support brackets. Position about 50 percent of support brackets to hit studs, but realize that wall clips don't need to go into studs.

installing closet components

Shelving systems, even do-it-yourself versions at hardware stores and home centers, now feature a bounty of storage accessories, such as sliding baskets, shoe racks, and scarf hangers. Consider the following before you pile on the special features.

Shop system first, accessories second. Some accessories are unique to specific brands, but many are very similar across systems. That said, don't try to blend elements from multiple systems; they're all just different enough to make mixing and matching tough.

Evaluate thoroughly. Just because you can doesn't mean you should. Rigorously question the function and usability of any storage accessories. The five shopping questions *on pages 28 and 29* will guide you to the right decision.

Anticipate interactions. You must have adequate room to operate accessories with moving parts. Envision the accessory filled with clothing. Are you still able to open the closet doors? Do long-hanging items get tangled in accessories below?

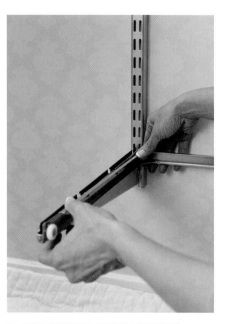

8. ADD SPECIALTY FEATURES
For drawers, start with the lowest one and affix the glide mechanism. Follow instructions for various bins and racks.

9. FINISH IT OFF
Drop bins or baskets into drawer frames. Cap shelves and exposed brackets with protective end pieces.

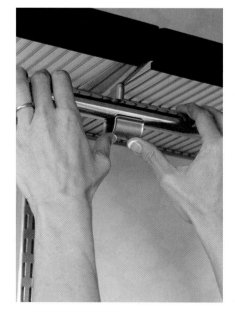

10. MOUNT RODS
Hang and secure clothing rods, following your system's specifications. Add extra support for spans longer than 36 inches.

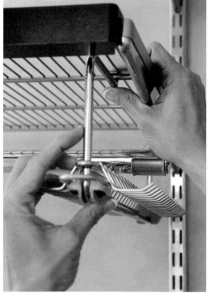

11. ENHANCE WITH ACCESSORIES
Explore options for storing belts, ties, shoes, and jewelry. Add organizers that fit your needs and budget.

Easy closet upgrades

If you lack the time or funds for a full-scale makeover, you can still enjoy a more organized wardrobe with quick, budget-friendly add-ons. Here are some of our favorites for any closet:

1 **Sliding rod tags** designate areas for specific types of clothing. Buy a set or make your own from pressboard.

2 **Flocked hangers** minimize garment slippage. They're also slim, so you can tuck in a few more items.

3 **Clip hangers** eliminate hanger creases on slacks and skirts.

4 **Plastic shelf liners** stop items from falling through slatted shelves and minimize imprints on folded clothing.

5 **Bins and baskets** are handy for rounding up bulky items such as blankets or serving as a drop spot for socks and delicates.

6 **Open shelves** provide the easiest access to shoes. Tight shelves are ideal for flats and sandals.

favorite storage shopping resources

Legend:
- ● Kitchens
- ● Living Spaces
- ● Personal Spaces
- ● Work Spaces

	Ballard Designs *ballarddesigns.com*	CB2 *cb2.com*	The Container Store *containerstore.com*	Crate & Barrel *crateandbarrel.com*	Great Useful Stuff *greatusefulstuff.com*	Hayneedle *hayneedle.com*	Home Decorators Collection *homedecorators.com*	IKEA *ikea.com*	Improvements *improvementscatalog.com*	JCPenney *jcpenney.com*	Kitchen Source *kitchensource.com*	The Land of Nod *landofnod.com*
Cabinet inserts & extras			●					●	●	●	●	
Food containers			●	●				●	●	●		
Islands				●		●	●	●		●	●	
Pantry accessories			●					●	●		●	
Accent tables	●	●		●		●	●	●		●	●	
Benches	●	●	●	●		●	●	●		●	●	●
Bookcases	●	●	●	●		●	●	●			●	●
Buffets and hutches	●	●		●		●	●	●			●	
Collectibles displays	●		●	●		●	●	●	●	●		●
Media solutions		●	●		●	●	●	●	●	●	●	
Armoires and dressers	●	●		●		●	●	●	●	●	●	●
Bars, hooks, and racks	●	●	●	●			●	●			●	
Clothing solutions	●	●	●	●	●			●	●	●		
Jewelry boxes & more	●		●		●	●		●	●	●		●
Linen closet add-ons	●	●	●	●				●	●		●	
Toiletry solutions	●	●	●	●				●				
Vanities		●	●			●	●	●			●	
Desks and work spaces	●	●	●	●	●	●	●	●	●	●	●	
Garage organizers			●	●	●	●		●	●		●	
Laundry organizers	●		●	●	●		●	●	●		●	●
Long-term storage			●					●	●			
Outdoor solutions		●	●	●		●		●	●	●	●	
Paper management	●	●	●	●	●			●				
Shelving	●	●	●		●	●	●	●			●	●

Organize.com organize.com	Organized A to Z organizedatoz.com	Organized Living organizedliving.com	Oxo oxo.com	PBTeen pbteen.com	Pottery Barn potterybarn.com	Rev-A-Shelf rev-a-shelf.com	Rubbermaid rubbermaid.com	Space Savers spacesavers.com	Stacks and Stacks stacksandstacks.com	Storables storables.com	Target target.com	Umbra umbra.com	West Elm westelm.com	World Market worldmarket.com
●	●	●				●	●	●	●	●	●			
●	●	●	●				●	●	●	●	●			●
								●			●			●
●	●	●	●			●	●	●	●	●		●		●
				●	●			●	●		●	●	●	●
●					●			●	●		●		●	●
●		●		●	●			●	●		●		●	●
●	●				●				●		●			●
●					●						●	●	●	
●		●		●	●			●	●	●	●		●	
●				●	●		●				●		●	
●	●	●	●					●	●		●	●		●
●	●	●				●		●			●			
●	●	●		●	●		●	●	●	●	●	●		
●	●	●	●	●	●	●	●	●	●	●	●			●
				●	●		●	●	●		●			
●					●			●	●	●	●		●	●
●	●	●	●	●				●	●	●	●			
●	●	●	●	●		●		●	●	●	●			●
●	●	●					●	●	●	●	●			
			●				●							
●	●	●	●	●	●			●	●	●	●			
●	●	●	●	●	●	●	●	●	●	●	●		●	●

contributing professional organizers

If you're stuck or can't get started, look to a professional organizer. These pros contributed their clutter-free insights to this book.

KATHY JENKINS, CPO
Come To Order, *cometoorderva.com*
Virginia-based organizer Kathy Jenkins created her business, Come To Order, to offer hands-on organizing support, workshops, seminars, and coaching services to busy families like hers. "Being organized isn't about rules," she says. "It's about doing the same thing time after time." In 2011, Jenkins created The Organizing Tutor, a study-habit program that offers parents an organizing assessment then delivers a customized report with recommendations to help students become more organized.

LAURA LEIST, CPO
Eliminate Chaos, *eliminatechaos.com*
Washington state–based organizer Laura Leist founded Eliminate Chaos in 2000 as an organizing and productivity-services. Clients include CEOs of multibillion-dollar corporations, high-profile authors, speakers, athletes, media personalities, and divas of domesticity. She's authored eight books and is the immediate past president of the National Association of Professional Organizers. She encourages clients to break projects into chunks, completing small tasks first. "You'll have the feeling of weight being lifted," Leist says. "Success is the biggest inspiration for further projects."

LORIE MARRERO, CPO
Clutter Diet, *clutterdiet.com*
In 2006, Lorie Marrero founded the revolutionary Clutter Diet online program, an affordable way for anyone to get expert organizing advice. Marrero serves as a spokesperson for Goodwill Industries International, and has served as a spokesperson for Staples, Microsoft, and other national media brands. As an active mother who has moved 11 times, Marrero brings tremendous insights into residential organizing, household management, and relocations. "Crash organizing doesn't work any better than crash dieting," Marrero says, "Unless you work on changing your habits, your space will quickly gain the clutter back."

"Purposeful storage feels less stressful: The muddy boots are in a pile. You can find your keys fast. You just feel good being in the space."
—Audrey Thomas

DONNA SMALLIN KUPER
The One-Minute Organizer, unclutter.com
Organizing expert Donna Smallin Kuper, founder of Unclutter.com and author of nine organizational help books, says flexibility is key in an efficient home. "Question everything!" Kuper says. "Just because you store something one way right now doesn't mean it has to be stored that way forever." Kuper received the 2006 Founders Award from NAPO for outstanding contributions to the industry and is frequently asked to serve as a brand spokesperson for leading manufacturers and service providers.

AUDREY THOMAS
Organized Audrey, organizedaudrey.com
Audrey Thomas, founder of Organized Audrey, works with business owners and employees frustrated by offices, in-boxes, and voice-mail systems overflowing with clutter. A believer in the "lean office," she encourages clients to assess needs before creating systems. "Shopping for organizing products happens last. First, sort, purge and see what you're left with," she says. "Think you need a new container? See if you already have something that will work. If not, only then should you go shopping." Thomas offers consulting services, employee coaching, and public speaking at seminars and workshops.

Find expert help, close to home

Start your search for a professional organizer in your area with the National Association of Professional Organizers. The membership-based organization is made up of 4,000 professional organizers who provide services to residential clients, small-business owners, special-needs customers, and midsize to large corporations. The NAPO website (*napo.net*) allows you to search for organizers by ZIP code, then follow links to professionals' websites for more information. The site also supplies tips on organizing homes and office spaces, time-management strategies, and relatable case studies.

Because professional organizer certification is not nationally regulated, NAPO membership is voluntary. However, members can become certified through NAPO's Certified Professional Organizer (CPO) program. CPOs have accumulated 1,500 hours of paid work and passed an exam. CPOs retain their credentials for three years and must earn continuing education credits to renew their certification.

"It's not my place to tell you what to keep or let go of, but I will hold up a mirror to what you're doing."
—Kathy Jenkins

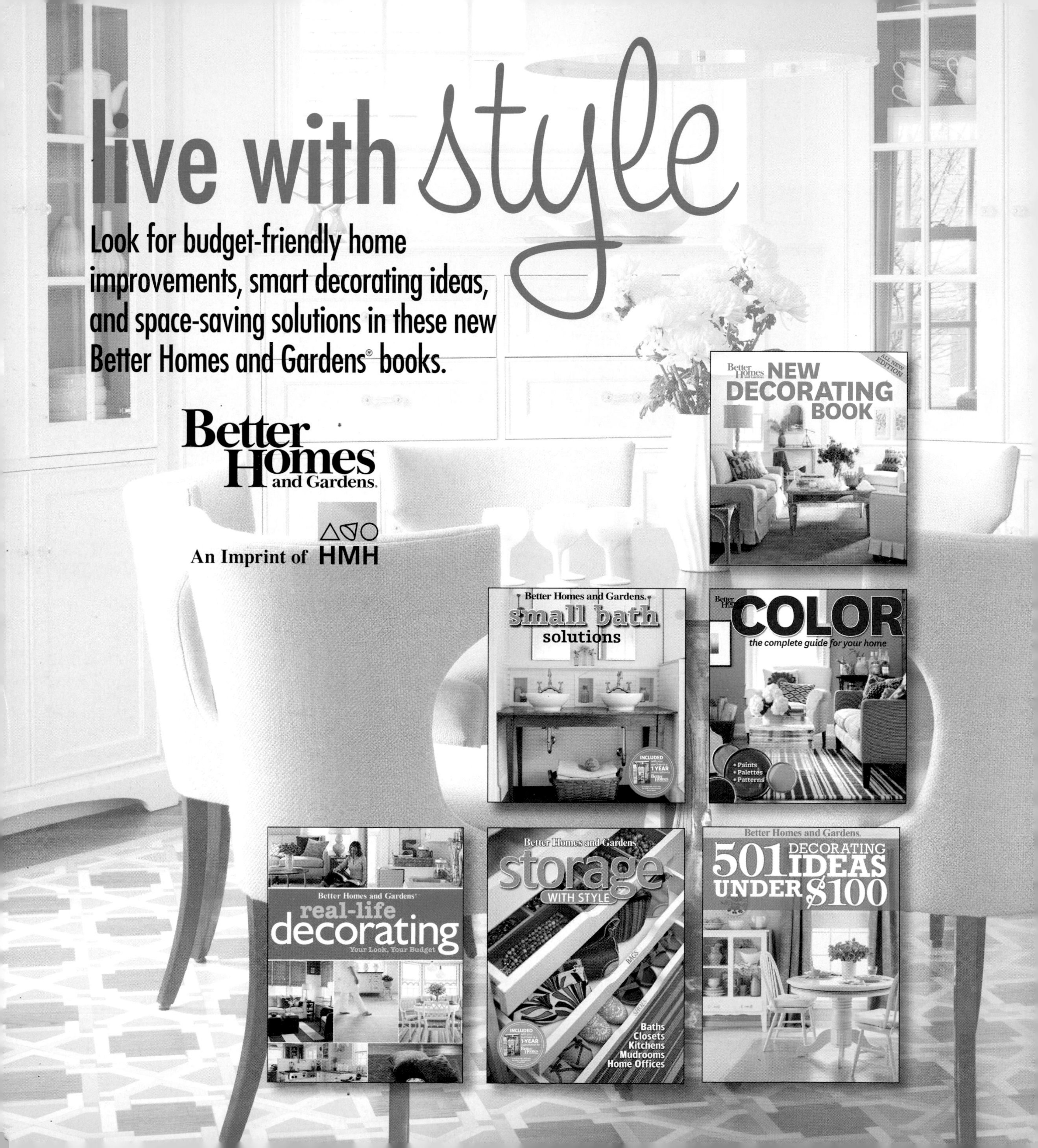

live with style
Look for budget-friendly home improvements, smart decorating ideas, and space-saving solutions in these new Better Homes and Gardens® books.
Better Homes and Gardens.
An Imprint of HMH
Better Homes and Gardens NEW DECORATING BOOK
ALL NEW EDITION
Better Homes and Gardens. small bath solutions
Better Homes and Gardens COLOR
the complete guide for your home
• Paints
• Palettes
• Patterns
Better Homes and Gardens real-life decorating
Your Look, Your Budget
Better Homes and Gardens storage WITH STYLE
Baths
Closets
Kitchens
Mudrooms
Home Offices
Better Homes and Gardens. 501 DECORATING IDEAS UNDER $100